FOREWORD BY *NEW YORK TIMES* BESTSELLING AUTHOR

CHRIS BRADY

FINANCIAL
FITNESS
FOR *Teens*

6 STEPS FROM
BROKE TO ABUNDANT

LIFE Leadership Essentials Series

OBSTACLÉS
PRESS

First Edition, October 2014
10 9 8 7 6 5 4 3 2 1

Published by:

Obstaclés Press
200 Commonwealth Court
Cary, NC 27511

lifeleadership.com

ISBN: 978-0-9904243-5-2

Cover design and layout by Norm Williams, nwa-inc.com

Printed in the United States of America

Sometimes it's only the young ones who are crazy enough to change the world.
—Diana Peterfreund

CONTENTS

FOREWORD

by Chris Brady

It's funny when I think about how many times during my school years I had the thought, "When am I *ever* going to *use* this?" Usually this was in response to an obscure math problem or complicated chemical equation that some teacher was intent on teaching me to balance. Indeed, by the end of my college years, I could work mathematical equations with virtuoso skill. Given a few minutes, I could reduce any equation down to the much sought after "zero equals zero." I remember manipulations of matrices, methods of integrations, and even friction cones as applied to robotic end effectors. And in my case, with the unpredictable path my life took from engineering to entrepreneurship and writing, I was correct in my suspicion that much of what I had been taught would go unused.

Don't get me wrong. I do not regret my formal education, and I've even made peace with the fact that I spent so many hours of my youth in the bowels of mathematical dungeons. I am not upset by all the learning I did that didn't end up being applicable in my life because, let's face it, there is no way to know exactly what will be useful later and what will not. And it was nobody's choice but my own to leave engineering for my true life's calling of being a business owner. But what I *do* wonder about, quite frankly, is all the stuff I *wasn't* taught along the way. At the top of that list is the topic of personal finance.

Why is it that we are taught the three Rs, "Reading, Riting, and Rithmetic," but nothing about money? Why must we dissect a frog but never learn to balance a checkbook? And why are some of us even taught macroeconomics but never *micro*economics, as in, *our own* economics?

The results of this oversight in education are predictable. The financial statistics for people in their twenties are dismal. Students graduate from high school and college, often laden with heavy student loan debt, and immediately get credit cards and car payments and frequently soon after, a mortgage. Just like that, they are buried under consumer debt. Unfortunately, this sets a pattern for life that is hard to break. And the load is difficult to bear. Interest on that debt compounds, and other forces like inflation work against them too. Add to this an overall ignorance about investing, and now our young people are not only having a hard time making ends meet, but what little is saved and stored someplace is done incorrectly. It all adds up to a life spent chasing after money to barely get by, when it didn't really have to be that way at all. What so many young people are missing as they start out in life is a foundation of financial wisdom.

Understanding money doesn't have to be hard. It isn't some great mystery, and it's certainly not boring. And for *sure*, nobody who ever learns the basics of good money management will *ever* have to ask themselves, "When will I ever use this?" Because the answer is obvious: Money is a topic, like it or not, that will be relevant in your life nearly every single day you are alive! It's best to understand it well and early. And that's the purpose of this book. Read on eagerly, and learn this stuff well. I promise you'll be glad you did!

WHY DON'T SCHOOLS TEACH THIS?

*Academic[s]…are important and so is
financial education. They're both important
and schools are forgetting one of them.*
—ROBERT KIYOSAKI

Will was angry. Actually, he didn't start out angry—
not at first. When he was sixteen years old, he decided
he wanted to graduate early from high school. With the
help of his parents, he enrolled in extra classes, took
high-school level courses through distance studies from
a university, and put in a lot of extra time reading,
studying, and learning.

On graduation night, the seniors in their caps and
gowns looked at him in surprise and asked, "What are
you doing here in line with us? You're only a junior."
Will just smiled.

He went to college and then got a good job working for
a Forbes 100 company. He also got married and started
raising a family.

A few years later, he came home one night and told his wife he really needed to talk.

"What's wrong?" she asked.

"Nothing, really," he replied. "I should be happy, but I'm just struggling." He sighed. "I know I should be really grateful that I have a good, steady job. And I am. I've been promoted twice, and to anyone else looking at my career, it would seem that I'm on the fast track to even more success."

Will paused. "But...I'm just not happy with my work. Is this all my life is about? Just going to work and spending my days earning cash by doing things my boss wants? I feel like I'm stuck in a rut, giving the best part of my life to my boss's priorities and interests.

"This just isn't what I dreamed of when I was in high school. I wanted to make a real difference in the world, to do something important—to do something great— and really help people."

Will's wife nodded. She'd seen him dealing with this struggle for quite a while.

"When I was growing up, I always thought I'd spend my life working for things that really matter. I saw so many men and women in my community who had kind of lost their dreams in life and spent all their time just working to pay the bills. I was sure I wouldn't become one of them. That's why I worked so hard to graduate a year early from high school. I couldn't wait to go out and really do something important in the world."

He paused again and looked up. "Yet here I am...."

She smiled with understanding and asked, "What do you want to do about it?"

Will sat up straight in his chair and responded, "I want to start looking for a better opportunity—something that I can get really excited about, something that will really help people."

Within a year, Will moved his family away from the Midwest to start a business in Colorado. He and his wife had looked around and studied a number of options, and they were excited to make the change. Two years later, they were so successful that they moved to Seattle, Washington, to expand their new business further.

During these years, Will was happy and excited about life. He woke up each morning full of enthusiasm for the projects of the day and went to bed at night tired but deeply fulfilled by what he had accomplished. He was helping lots of people! It was just what he had dreamed of when he was a teenager.

Then the economy went through a major recession, the number of his clients and buyers dwindled, and on the week of his fortieth birthday, he finally closed his business for good. When he locked the front doors of the now empty business building and walked to his car, he wasn't sure what lay ahead for him. Like the night of his graduation from high school, he knew he was beginning a new phase in his life, but he wasn't sure what it might look like.

Will and his family moved back to Missouri to be close to relatives. The first week there, some friends introduced him to an opportunity that would enable him to own his own business through an already-established system so he wouldn't have to spend his time on all the entrepreneurial startup grunt work. He and his wife jumped at the chance. As part of the process, he started reading the book *Financial Fitness: The Offense, Defense, and Playing Field of Personal Finance*.[1] He also listened to several audios that came in the mail with the book.

After he read the first three chapters one afternoon, he began feeling upset. As he continued reading, he became downright angry. He stomped around the house for two days telling everyone who would listen how frustrated he was. "Why didn't anyone ever teach me these things before?" he fumed. "Why didn't someone, anyone, teach me this when I was young? It just doesn't make sense. Why didn't I learn this in high school or even middle school—or at least in college? My life would be so much better right now if I had known these things when I was thirteen, fourteen, or sixteen."

Will kept reading the book and listening to the audios—and ranting to everyone he saw—until, after several days, he realized the anger was gone.

In its place, he found hope and excitement.

As he read, he realized something that made him stop, lean back in his chair, and smile widely. "It's not too late!" he said aloud, though nobody else was in the room to hear him. But the words were important, so he said them again, slowly, to himself: "It's not too late!"

His mind started racing: *It's not too late to start applying the financial principles I'm learning. I wish I had learned them earlier, but since I didn't, I'll just start applying them now.*

His new business gave him an excellent opportunity to apply the principles of financial fitness in a way that could make him really successful while also helping him serve people and make a difference in the world. He was only forty, he told himself, and now was the perfect time to learn and utilize the principles of successful entrepreneurship and financial fitness.

Just imagine what could have happened if he had learned these principles twenty-five years earlier when he was a teenager....

Financial Education Is Too Often Lacking!

Have you ever noticed that most schools don't teach much about money? Granted, throughout elementary and middle school, and even more in the high school and college years, there's a lot taught about the importance of getting a good job or career later in life, and a job or career that involves more money is generally considered better than one that earns less. But when it comes to the real principles of financial fitness, most schools have very little—if anything at all—to say. And the little they do teach is often just plain wrong.

This is interesting, since it's not exactly an unimportant topic. In fact, it is extremely important. Almost everyone who reaches adulthood wishes he or she had learned more about finances sooner in life.

If you were to go around asking forty-year-olds, fifty-year-olds, and sixty-year-olds what they wish they had known more about earlier in life, "money smarts" would be one of the top answers.

In fact, when adults *do* stumble across positive financial education in their later years, many respond just as Will did, asking, "Why didn't anyone tell me this sooner?!" Even the less resentful responses often run along the lines of "I could have been so much more successful by now if I had only known and applied these things."

For some, it goes as far as "I could have been a millionaire or a successful business owner five times over if I had known these financial principles earlier in life."

There certainly isn't a lack of demand for financial education, and everyone could benefit greatly from understanding even a few basic financial principles and ideas just a little bit better.

Financial fitness is one of the most important things a person can learn in life! Real financial savvy is something that can absolutely transform an individual's ability to achieve and even correctly pursue success. It also significantly impacts the way we see and interact with others and, ultimately, the contribution we make to society.

And the earlier we learn and start living by wise financial principles, the more success we can achieve.

When children and teenagers learn and apply these principles, it puts them way ahead in life. Fortunately, with this book, you can be one of these "way ahead" people yourself!

FINANCIAL FITNESS MATTERS!

People who understand the principles of financial fitness are not only more often successful individuals, but they also have the potential to be much better citizens and more powerful leaders in the world.

Those who don't understand money and what makes it tick miss out on the opportunity to serve and lead in powerful ways. They often end up being slaves to their money, sometimes to the point of *hurting* society, and certainly themselves, in big ways. Not to mention, it is no fun to be the guy who can never make it financially, simply because he doesn't know the principles of success.

> **People who understand the principles of financial fitness are not only more often successful individuals, but they also have the potential to be much better citizens and more powerful leaders in the world.**

Yet, as we've said, most schools simply do not teach the principles of financial fitness. Some might say that this is because they feel it's the role of parents to teach these concepts, and they don't want to step on any toes. But schools teach many things that used to belong to the domain of parents and families. Perhaps it's because they think kids don't have or care about money yet, so it won't be applicable until later; they'll get it in college or some other time. It's also possible that they think it's not an important topic. But maybe, since many educators were never taught very much on the subject themselves, they simply feel ill-equipped to address it.

Whatever the reason, the result is that in most cases, teens are simply not receiving the kind of financial preparation that is vitally important to their success, information that would give them a huge leg up in life and is more helpful, more powerful, and just plain *better* the earlier it's learned.

This lack of preparation is expensive in more ways than one. And unfortunately, by the time most people realize that they don't know enough of the right information about financial fitness (and some never do), they have often missed opportunities and mishandled situations that could have put them in a great financial position or kept them out of big financial troubles. Of course by this point, they may have already raised their kids with the wrong financial information, duplicating if not multiplying their own unhappy results for future generations.

Clearly, this is a huge problem, but the solution is just as big and actually relatively simple to implement. We just need to get the right information into the right hands! That's where *you* come in.

The beauty of the whole problem is that *you* have all the power to fix this situation in your own life—in a way that will influence those around you and impact generations to come.

If the *problem* is that the youth aren't getting the right financial education, then the *solution* is for you, the youth, to start getting it! This might seem daunting or difficult, but you're in the right place! Keep reading. Learning and understanding the basics of financial fitness in your youth and implementing them right from the beginning will give you a huge advantage over your parents' generation—not to mention the head start it will give your children and grandchildren to follow.

> **If the *problem* is that the youth aren't getting the right financial education, then the *solution* is for you, the youth, to start getting it!**

THE SIX STEPS

This book will teach you six steps you can take right now—as you move toward adulthood and begin your financial journey—to improve your overall financial success and your ability to make a positive difference in the world and live a happy, productive, successful, and truly meaningful life.

Education is in many ways the primary difference between success and failure in finances in general—and, in fact, in most aspects of life. Having the right information and, more important, the right *thinking* will make all the difference in how you approach life and what kind of results you achieve. By the time you finish this book, you'll know more about financial fitness (and how to actually achieve it in a simple, consistent way) than nearly all the adults you'll ever meet. That's exciting, but the great thing is that as you apply the principles you'll

> **Having the right information and, more important, the right *thinking* will make all the difference in how you approach life and what kind of results you achieve.**

read about in this book, you'll become financially fit. This will bring you increased peace, success, and opportunity.

As you learn the right information, adopt the right mindset, and then apply these in your approach to money, you will be on the path to real success, since you'll be learning where to start, what to do, whom to follow, and how to stay on track and make necessary course corrections and adjustments.

Start Now!

There is power in good financial education, and starting at a young age increases it exponentially!

You probably aren't in a major financial rut just yet, and wouldn't you like it to stay that way? So many adults would jump at the chance to be simply "broke" again, rather than dealing with mountains of debt and difficulty and the bad financial habits they've built up with the wrong financial information. By starting now, you can avoid all such problems entirely.

You're in a great place! You have all the power to get the right mentors, information, and financial mindset before you make any huge and life-altering mistakes.

You have the power to get the financial education that'll set you up for life, and you're likely doing it with a blank slate—no marks against you. Naturally, you may still face some financial challenges, setbacks, and difficulties, but having the right understanding and approach to money will make them all much less painful and a whole lot more fruitful in the long run.

Learning and applying the principles of financial fitness that are taught in this book will enable you to take yourself from financially broke to financially free, independent, and truly abundant in life!

Whether you're a child or a teen (or an adult) reading this, we know you can handle the real information, so we won't try to dumb it down or sugarcoat anything. We know you need to receive the whole picture now, without pulled punches or overly simplified general-izations. You've probably had enough of dumbed-down short sentences meant to keep you quiet for a few more years, until it will be somebody else's problem to help you learn what you need to know to be truly financially fit and successful.

We're confident you can handle the deep stuff, and we want to give you the tools you need to start your journey in the right direction and with the right energy.

So let's get started on the six steps from "broke to abundant"! As you learn these, you'll be on a path few people ever take. And you'll be doing it in your youth!

UNDERSTANDING MONEY

FOCUS ON THE BASICS

Civilised life, you know, is based on a huge number of illusions in which we all collaborate willingly. The trouble is we forget after a while that they are illusions and we are deeply shocked when reality is torn down around us.
—J. G. BALLARD

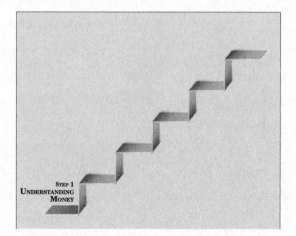

Before you can really get into the nitty-gritty details and techniques of financial fitness, it's crucial to start with the correct overall view of money and finances. It's important to see the whole picture, to understand money itself, before you try to strategize and plan how to most effectively make or use it. When you *don't* understand the basic rules and nature of money, you're bound to make a bunch of mistakes with it, simply because you don't know what you're doing.

On the flipside, when you really understand money, knowing the techniques and strategies that work best will only add to your financial savvy and increase your ability to make money work in the best ways for you and your purpose.

> **When you really understand money, knowing the techniques and strategies that work best will only add to your financial savvy and increase your ability to make money work in the best ways for you and your purpose.**

SEEING THE FOREST, THE TREES, *AND* THE OCEAN

Unfortunately, in the words of bestselling author Chris Brady, "Most people are terrible at money!" Likewise, their role models were also terrible at money. Fortunately, you don't have to follow in the footsteps of tradition. Nor do you need to believe, as many do, that seeking to achieve a higher financial education or even a better financial situation is unrealistic, materialistic, and possibly even greedy.

In fact, this path of deliberately avoiding reality and consciously choosing not to better your financial environment and situation is exactly what leads to most materialism and money-driven action. As Oscar Wilde put it, "There is only one class in the community that thinks more about money than the rich, and that is the poor."[1]

Sadly, for many who don't have a realistic view of financial fitness, life frequently becomes all about money. As long as they never have it, they continue to chase it.

Instead of providing examples of questioning, seeking answers, and *learning* what money is and how to be good at managing it, some parents, teachers, and other role models instead leave children and youth to assume the world is just "tough like that." The reality, according to them, seems to be: "Others can make it financially because they were lucky, but in our family [community, class, etc.], this is the rut we get. So make the most of it and just enjoy the hard work, debt, and eternal financial stress." Tragically, since no one and nothing—including their own experience—ever tells or demonstrates to these young people otherwise, this is what they end up believing.

Just as a quick reminder, in case you're getting caught up in the cynicism and hopelessness of a financial viewpoint and educational approach that is fundamentally wrong, this is a bad way to view money, and it's really not a good way to decide how you're going to view money!

INHERENT LESSONS AND THE OBVIOUS

For example, during a special career week a school was sponsoring, a young schoolteacher was assigned to hold a discussion in class on how to choose a career path. She prepared diligently and arrived at school that morning ready to teach the students about this very important topic.

She began by explaining that really, the only option was to graduate from college with good grades and pursue a stable job.

One particularly rambunctious student raised his hand and listed four or five successful entrepreneurs, artists, and business owners (some of whom were even college dropouts) who had actually made a lot more money than the average employee could ever hope for. Then he asked about the lessons of these examples. To his amazement, her unflinching response was to say the lesson was very clear. "They could do that, and how lucky for them, but the rest of us need to pursue good degrees and stable jobs."

The boy realized that the kind of success and results achieved by the people on his list came with a masive amount of hard work. Clearly the teacher was saying that it would be less risky to seek a job rather than to try to make it big on your own. But he was shocked to hear her say that the actual lesson we learn from the success of others is that *they* can do it, but *we* can't. *What?* Where on earth was she getting that?

He decided she must have misspoken, or perhaps she just knew more on the topic, so he pushed her a bit further. His parents had built a successful entrepreneurial business that allowed them to eventually leave their jobs and earn great success. So he knew from their example that what the teacher was saying simply wasn't accurate.

"You mean the principle we learn from the lives of Benjamin Franklin, Will Smith, Steve Jobs, Oprah Winfrey, Andrew Carnegie, Ralph Lauren, Mark Zuckerberg, and others like them is that it's *impossible* to come from low circumstances and achieve great financial success?" Half laughing at the ridiculousness of his question, he tried to make himself as clear as possible, so she'd be sure to contradict him and explain what she *really* meant.

The teacher looked at him for a moment before giving him a sympathetic smile. Then she repeated her assurances that their luck was "good for them" but it taught that the rest of us have to work hard at a typical job in order to *hope* to make ends meet until retirement.

When the young man protested, sharing his dream to work hard and become an entrepreneur and a millionaire, she laughed at him outright and finally concluded the class by commenting sarcastically, "Well, good luck with that!"

"But my parents did it," he told her. "And so did many of their friends." She was surprised but had no answer.

While some teachers do understand and pass on important principles of financial fitness, this unfortunate tale is one that occurs far more often than it should.

For most people, however, the topic of how money works isn't addressed directly at all, which means it is unconsciously, even *accidently*, learned. And when it is brought up, it's usually set aside as quickly as possible with a few bold and incorrect statements about "the way things are," and that's the end of it.

In other words, whatever young people's financial surroundings teach, they tend to believe for themselves, combined with a pinch of blind hope that everything will work out in the best way possible—which probably won't happen, unless they learn and apply the principles of financial fitness.

With this approach, if you grew up in a forest, you think the whole world is a forest. ("It's all trees.") If you grew up in the city, the world is just a big city. If you grew up in the mountains, mountains it is.

WHAT THE WORLD'S MADE OF

Of course, you're smart enough to know that the world is made up of many different environments. We have mountains, forests, deserts, oceans, plains, and so on. Money also has various components and aspects to understand. We need to look at a much larger picture than just our own circumstances. The whole world is *not* a forest. Period. Therefore, viewing it as such is an absolute failure to comprehend the big picture—or reality. No matter how long you have to walk before you see the end of the trees, the end *is* there. There *are* cities, oceans, mountains, and plains. The world is *not* just a forest. End of story.

And since it doesn't work to just go with what you see in front of you and assume you understand the world—like the guy who couldn't see the forest for the trees—some additional digging and education on the big picture is needed to understand money and to see why that teacher was wrong.

> **No matter how long you have to walk before you see the end of the trees, the end *is* there.**

If people don't understand true principles, it's amazing what absurdities they'll adopt as fact.

Unfortunately, the truth of this statement is easy to see in the way most people view and perceive money and success. All you have to do is look around. Everywhere, people who believe all sorts of absurdities are passing them on to others and making some of their most important life decisions based on the same ridiculous financial fallacies.

> **If people don't understand true principles, it's amazing what absurdities they'll adopt as fact.**

A broader and deeper understanding of the *real* picture of what money is (and what it isn't) is sorely needed in our world—and fast. It's up to you to get your hands on the right information as early as possible and start applying and spreading it right now! That's why reading this book is so important.

As you come to understand money and treat it in the right ways, you'll be making a huge difference in your own future while also preparing yourself to pass on the proper mindset to posterity to stop the generations-old trend of being absolutely terrible with money! The fact that you have this book probably means your parents have learned or are learning the principles of financial fitness and can help you on your journey.

UNDERSTANDING YOUR ROLE

When it comes to having the right thinking about money, one of the first things you should understand is that money is a stewardship. The word *stewardship* is both interesting and vital because it incorporates two very important ideas into one.

The first idea incorporated in stewardship is that

> **The first idea incorporated in stewardship is that money is a *blessing*.**

money is a *blessing*. It's a huge benefit when it comes, whether from your parents or your own hard work. Either way, be grateful for it. Money is abundant and valuable, and it ultimately comes to you as a blessing from God as you work hard and do your part.

As a steward, you are *blessed* with money, which can be a tremendous benefit and resource. It is potential energy that gives you incredible leverage and opportunity and allows you to accomplish things that would be much more difficult without it.

This "blessing" part of stewardship is really important and, honestly, pretty cool.

Likely, you know the word *steward* from *The Lord of the Rings*,[2] since the ruler of Gondor before Aragorn's return is called a "steward." In this case, we tend to think of it as merely another name they gave their ruler instead of king, like a prime minister or a president, but this idea of who a steward is and what he does gives us a great picture of the "blessing" part of the word. Clearly the steward of Gondor was blessed by the situation.

Interestingly, Denethor himself does a great job of introducing the other important aspect of stewardship by showing us what *not* to do! You see, while the position of steward was traditionally one that involved much blessing, power, and opportunity, it was nevertheless the position of a higher-ranking *servant*. That's right; a steward isn't just a fancy-coated ruler. He is a servant to

> **The second idea included in the concept of stewardship is that money is a *responsibility*.**

a higher master (in this case, the kings of Gondor),

charged with caring for and overseeing his lord's houses, lands, people, etc. in his absence.

Therefore, the second idea included in the concept of stewardship is that money is a *responsibility*. Stewards are not simply heirs who inherit wealth and get to waste it in whatever way they choose. Not at all.

In fact, along with enjoying the blessings of money, stewards are primarily responsible for using that money in specific ways to fulfill a certain purpose, as given by the master.

In short, as a steward of money, you have to understand that you are truly blessed to have it! Be excited at the potential energy you've received and earned in this powerful resource. But at the same time, remember that

> **Money comes with a responsibility to use it wisely and rightly.**

how you use it matters and that wasting it is not a good plan. Money comes with a responsibility to use it wisely and rightly.

As the steward of Gondor, Denethor had the ability and authority to order his son and all his soldiers to do bad things that hurt many people, even though he had a responsibility *not* to. The point? Don't be that kind of steward. Choose instead to be a good steward of money throughout your life, using it for beneficial and useful purposes. This is your decision to make—and one you should stick to.

MENTORING MATTERS!

As you're probably aware by now, it's crucial that you don't decide what kind of a steward you will be based on the habits you've seen or the unconscious training you've received from everyone around you. Listen only to those who are good at handling money.

This is incredibly important! Learn from those who really know what you want to learn. In the case of money, learn from those who are financially fit themselves. Find good financial mentors who are excellent stewards of their money.

After the responsibility of stewardship, the need for a good mentor is probably the second most important thing to understand as you establish your thinking about money.

A mentor is a trusted adviser who's there to help you along your journey. It's someone who's ahead of you on the journey and has already achieved the results you're hoping for in the area he or she mentors you in. The idea is that, since this person has already been where you are and faced many of the same challenges and difficulties that will come up in your life, he or she is able to help you make better decisions, avoid unnecessary mistakes and pain, and find the best shortcuts and smartest ways to work in order to achieve optimum results.

Mentoring is huge! You know by now that financial fitness, and therefore a good financial education, is a big deal, and you also know a lot of places you shouldn't go looking for it. Now it's time to talk about where you *should* go to get the right kind of education on money and learn the strongest principles of financial fitness.

It's actually quite simple.

To repeat: Seek counsel from mentors (through a combination of in-person consultations, audios, and books) who actually have the kind of financial results you're looking for. In other words, as we said in the book *Financial Fitness,* "Stop getting financial advice from broke people!"[3]

You need advice and guidance, since there's a lot you don't know yet, and you don't even know what you don't know. But please, learn from people who are genuinely qualified to teach you. The concept is called "fruit on the tree": you should not seek advice about how to grow fruit from those with barren trees.

Unfortunately, a lot of people think having done it wrong and suffered greatly makes them qualified to advise you. This is simply not the case; empty branches, empty advice. Their stories may give you extra motivation to seek out the right information from those who actually have it, since—as they'll tell you again and again—you don't want to end up like them.

> **Unfortunately, a lot of people think having done it wrong and suffered greatly makes them qualified to advise you. This is simply not the case.**

Still, they should not be the place you look for the

answers to your questions or the path to success, since they don't really know and haven't achieved it yet. It's good to learn from the mistakes of those who aren't financially fit, but don't assume that knowing one way that *doesn't* work makes them experts on what *does* work.

This is blunt, but it's vitally important to your financial success. You should certainly love and appreciate people, no matter how poor their finances, and even listen to their advice in areas where they've achieved the results you're looking for. But if you don't want what they have financially, then don't follow their financial choices or counsel.

That said, when you find mentors who have actually achieved the financial results you want, it's important that you learn as much from them as you can as soon as you can and actually do what they say!

When you've found the right mentor, you should be such a nag that he or she tells you it's too much! Not only does this mean asking so many questions and trying to get so much advice that the mentor has to tell you you're too hungry. It also means *applying* everything you're told immediately and consistently.

You don't want to be the kind of mentee who expects the mentor to teach you everything and do the work too! Be the kind of protégé who hungrily and consistently seeks your mentor's guidance and then applies it all perfectly, exactly, and immediately before going back for the next step.

If you're getting the right financial information from the right sources, and then you're actually *applying* it, you will experience positive, real results in your finances and in life. This book is a powerful place to get such information. It in itself is a form of mentorship, and it (and other resources like it) may be all the mentoring you can find for a while. That's okay. Just gobble up the information and start using it right away.

This is the best way to shape your thinking on money, and it will help you in countless other ways as you learn and apply the principles of good mentoring. That's why we wrote this book: to teach the many lessons on financial fitness outlined by two very successful business leaders, Chris Brady and Orrin Woodward.

For more on how to really get the most out of your mentors, we refer you to the excellent book *Mentoring Matters*.[4] To learn more about financial fitness, keep reading!

DOING PURPOSE ON PURPOSE

In all this, keep one thing in mind. Yes, getting the right kind of financial thinking and information, getting the right mentors, and ultimately getting *good* at applying the principles of financial fitness can really help you live happily and fulfill your life purpose.

> **Life is not about money, and money does *not* equal happiness or success.**

However, money is *not* the point of your life.

Remember this: life is not about money, and money does *not* equal happiness or success.

One of the most important parts of understanding money is knowing that as a steward of money, your life *does* have a point, and while money can really help—and a lack of money will probably really hurt—money is not your great purpose. Money is a stewardship and a responsibility that's all about helping you better fulfill your life mission and purpose.

> **Purpose and happiness aren't about money. Money is about furthering your purpose and happiness.**

In other words, purpose and happiness aren't about money. Money is about furthering your purpose and happiness, and it's only helpful or good to the exact extent that it's serving these higher priorities.

No matter how prosperous or even wealthy you become, you will never be truly happy or even really successful if you are not aligned with your God-given life purpose. As you learn the techniques and principles of making money work better for you, don't forget that it is simply a tool to help you achieve the things in life that matter most.

> **No matter how prosperous or even wealthy you become, you will never be truly happy or even really successful if you are not aligned with your God-given life purpose.**

Keep learning, always maintaining the proper perspective and self-discipline to fully *live* the right financial principles. That way, you will be shaping the kind of financial future that enables you to live your dreams, accomplish your purpose in life, and change the world in powerful and magnificent ways.

Capitalize on your youth, and make the small financial changes and habits *now* that will make an enormous difference in your future.

Understanding money is really *that* important, and the consequences are really *that* big. Every one of you young men and women in this fight needs to understand money and make it work for you in the best possible ways. Achieving your own success is a small price to pay.

Not to mention, you *don't* want to end up like Denethor.

STEP 1 SUMMARY
Understanding Money

1. It is incredibly important to get a financial education and understand the principles of financial fitness.

2. There are six steps from broke to abundant, and the first step is to understand the principles of financial fitness.

3. Learn financial fitness from those who have the kind of financial success you want (not from people who are broke).

4. Money is a stewardship, meaning you have a responsibility to use it wisely in fulfilling your life purpose.

5. Money is a blessing. Even though you work hard for it, always be grateful.

6. As you learn from good financial mentors (including this book), you must do more than listen or read. You must immediately and consistently *apply* the principles and techniques you learn!

7. Money does not equal success or happiness, but it can help you fulfill your life purpose more successfully and joyfully.

8. Financial fitness is a vital part of a wise and happy life.

9. Remember these principles and make them part of your everyday thinking about money and financial fitness.

MAKING MONEY

THE OWNERSHIP RULE:
OWNERS RULE

Money is better than poverty, if
only for financial reasons.
—WOODY ALLEN

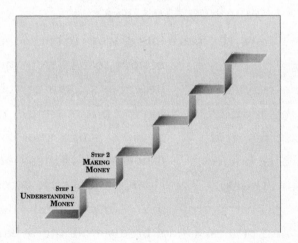

The next step is to actually have some money yourself. Just like it's not time to strategize how to make money until you've got a wider view of things, it's somewhat pointless to plan how to save, invest, or spend money until you actually have some.

Of course, you should know these principles before you get to the point of having to make big decisions, if you can. But starting at the beginning and taking the steps in the right order will prepare you to face the world of money in a much better way than simply bopping around learning random financial facts and fads that present themselves on TV shows or Facebook. Even the good and right things should be learned in the right ways, at the right times, and with the right perspective.

So once you've got the right "moneyview" (as Chris Brady calls it), it's time to learn the best ways to get some actual money to work with!

BAD TO GOOD; GOOD TO GREAT

As you know, there are lots of ways to get money, even in your teens—from mowing a neighbor's lawn to robbing a bank to babysitting or running a bake sale, and countless others. But as these examples clearly illustrate, some ways are simply and naturally better than others. Undoubtedly, robbing a bank is a bad financial decision. The years in prison will set back anyone's finances a long, long way. Plus, it's wrong. One of the first principles of financial fitness is that you only want money you've obtained honestly.

> **Some ways of getting money are simply and naturally better than others.**

And it goes further than "ethical trumps unethical." While it's fairly obvious to most people that coming by your money through honest means is better than stealing, cheating, or otherwise swindling, there are actually a few other lines that separate bad ways to make money from good ones, though we think this is a pretty good place to start.

Being honest and ethical is a vitally important principle of success and achievement, since no matter how much money you can manage to make through dishonest and unethical behavior, your overall happiness and even your ability to sustain a positive financial situation under such circumstances will be unstable at best and probably nonexistent at worst. Make your money honestly, and you'll be a lot happier in life. You'll keep your integrity, which matters a lot more than money.

Frankly, it's probably obvious to you that making a bad choice is not nearly as good as making a good one. With that understood, let's jump into the next point.

In reality, the gap between *good* ways to make money and *great* ways to make money is pretty big, and this distinction is very important to those who hope to achieve great success and make a positive difference in the world.

GREAT INCOME FACTOR #1: PURPOSE FIRST

As Carlos Ruiz Zafón wrote in *The Shadow of the Wind*, "Making money isn't hard in itself....What's hard is to earn it doing something worth devoting one's life to."[1] While we recognize the truth of his remark—it does take real effort to make money doing your mission and living your dreams—we maintain that it *is* still worth it and that it should be your aim. It just may take a while to get there.

Many people decide to sacrifice what they see as their true potential, even their "calling in life," simply because it's too hard or because they feel they can't afford it. This is a real problem and causes a lot of pain and heartache for many people. Still, there is a solution: fight for something that matters, realizing it might take some time.

Let's be clear. Doing so can and will be hard—perhaps the hardest thing you ever do. But not only is it a good thing; it's the only thing. Consider the alternative. Getting what you want is hard. But you don't want anything else, so you'd better get to work!

> **Getting what you want is hard. But you don't want anything else, so you'd better get to work!**

At some point, you're going to have to find a way to leverage your time, your talent, your money, or something else so that it brings you income. We're suggesting that the best way to do this is to find some means of leveraging your *purpose* to do so.

It isn't bad to have a burger-flipping job in high school or a landscaping job over the summer to bring in a little extra cash to pay for your new bicycle. But beyond that, it's a good idea for you to start looking toward an income-making opportunity and situation as early as possible that involves you living your dreams and contributing to society in really important ways. You want to be a "producer."

This is how *New York Times* bestselling author Oliver DeMille describes producers in his book *FreedomShift*: "Producers create and add value to society and mankind. Thus, they are the most important people in an economy or nation."[2] And focusing on connecting your own income to what you have to add to the world is not only true and excellent entrepreneurship but also usually the best way to make a difference and live a fulfilling and happy life. It will give you a great advantage as well because, as Orrin Woodward puts it, your *passion* will be connected to your *profits*.

Again, we're not saying this is the only way you should make money or that you should sit around mooching off the work of others while you await a perfect opportunity to make money doing what you love. That would be the exact opposite of what we're saying. But even as you're making money in summer jobs and the like, you should be looking toward a future of profits pursued in line with your passions.

> "Producers create and add value to society and mankind. Thus, they are the most important people in an economy or nation."
> —Oliver DeMille

In fact, as long as you keep your eyes on the prize and constantly look for and take opportunities to get closer and closer to the goal, every little job you have can teach you valuable lessons that will prepare you for where you want to be and make you better at fulfilling your own purpose.

This is the first distinguishing factor between good income and great income: purpose. You have a life purpose; eventually you'll need to find a way to make your purpose make your living. It's never too early for you to start thinking about and planning for this. (For more clarity and direction on this topic, please see the first two chapters of Chris Brady's bestselling book *PAiLS*.[3])

Great Income Factor #2: Own Your Income

The second factor of *great* income is also important and valuable, but it absolutely comes *after* the first and will apply differently to different people based on the first. Still, it's an essential principle of financial fitness, and understanding it so you can apply it to your own mission and life purpose is both helpful and important. The principle is *ownership*.

As much as possible, it is better to own your income than to be dependent on others for it. Therefore, in most cases, you want to seek to own your own business rather than having a job working for someone else. We admit, it can be hard to make much income early on doing this, and it's great to shovel some driveways along the way as well. But don't let the challenge stop you from pursuing it because for most people, business ownership over employment is half the battle to a great life purpose versus randomly acquired cash to pay your bills.

Knowing your purpose and counseling with a mentor who understands your unique situation will allow you to make these decisions in the way that best fits your needs. Other things being equal, in general, you're more likely to fund your life purpose— between having the right resources and enjoying the necessary freedom and time— as a successful business owner than as an employee. This is

> **Knowing your purpose and counseling with a mentor who understands your unique situation will allow you to make decisions in the way that best fits your needs.**

the reality! So start working toward this as early as possible in your financial journey.

Naturally, we understand that you will not actually be starting your own business at this exact moment, but having this mindset will help you start moving in the right direction. And knowing that this is what you are aiming at will help you take the steps needed to get you there at the right time. You'll be watching for instead of missing the opportunities or lessons that will be pivotal to your overall success when it *is* time to build your own business.

In fact, the earlier you understand this and prepare for it, the easier it will be to achieve success on the path of ownership. This is true whatever kind of business and mission you choose to build in your life. For instance, even if your goal is to be a doctor, a lawyer, an accountant, or an engineer, the most successful people in these careers own their own firms and practices—because this gives them more time and resources to really focus on improving the world. Let's look at Eliza as an example.

THE WORD ON ELIZA'S BACK

Eliza attended a youth conference in the summer, and it was a life-changing experience for her. She had been to youth conferences before, but this one was even more amazing than usual. On the first day, a speaker handed out pieces of paper and some tape and had everybody post a sheet on the back of their shirts.

Then she gave them black markers and had them go to different people and write one word on each person's paper. "Write the word that for you best describes this person," she told them.

Eliza participated, writing various words on her classmates' papers and having them write on her back as well. When the speaker had them pull the papers off their backs and read what their peers had written about them, Eliza had a powerful experience.

The first word she noticed on her paper once she had it in front of her really made her mind reel. The word was *deep*.

Eliza was shocked. *Am I deep?* she wondered. She had never really thought of herself in that way. The other words were more expected: *sweet, loving, nice...* and even *elegant*. But *deep*? Tears filled her eyes.

When Eliza got home after the conference, she showed the paper to her dad. His first response was "Wow! One of your words is *deep*! That's so great...and so *true*. Eliza, you really are amazingly deep. I don't know how the other person saw this so quickly, but it's true."

"Actually, Dad," Eliza responded, "I couldn't wait to get home and discuss this with you. As I've told you many times, my career goal is to be a successful business owner, but I've always wondered if I was smart enough or strong enough to succeed. When I read *deep* on my paper at the conference, something just clicked inside me, and I knew I never needed to doubt myself that way again. I really do have the depth to live my dreams and achieve my goals, don't I?"

"Absolutely, you do," he responded immediately.

"Oh," she continued, "one of the other speakers was a successful entrepreneur who said that the keys to his success are the ABCs of leadership: Attitude, Belief, and Commitment. Since I know that my career plan is entrepreneurship, I was able to personally connect with everything he talked about. In fact, this was true for all the speakers. It's like every class, book, or speaker I encounter is teaching me how to achieve my goals someday—and how to get started right now. I worry about the other students, at least those who don't know their adult goals yet, because they couldn't possibly have learned as much."

GREAT INCOME FACTOR #3: THE GIFT THAT KEEPS ON GIVING

A third factor is closely connected to the second (and, like business ownership, should also be considered in the context of your life purpose). However, it includes an important nuance that will provide perspective and direction for your goals and dreams as you set out to be financially fit and successful.

This third factor is *residual income*. Just as you should be consistently looking toward making your income as large as needed to fulfill your purpose, and in a way that's actually connected to that purpose, generally through business ownership, seeking *residual* forms of income rather than simple *one-time payments* should be a priority in the way you approach moneymaking.

Residual income is money that continues to pay you again and again after the original work is done. Examples would include an author's royalties on a book he wrote once, the money the electric company gets from hundreds of thousands of people whose houses it set up to receive service three decades ago, or any of the hundreds of subscription-based systems where a salesperson sold a family once on the product and gets a commission every month from their magazine, security system, or television service.

In his book *Cashflow Quadrant*,[4] *New York Times* bestselling author Robert Kiyosaki uses the example of building a pipeline as opposed to carrying individual buckets to and from the well to get your water. When you have a pipeline set up, getting water into your home is a much simpler process than when you have to carry buckets, and it allows you to spend your time doing the things you love and care about most instead of being tied to your buckets in order to fulfill your family's basic need for water.

When you have money flowing into your life on a residual basis, you'll be able to spend your time doing what you were born to do, fulfilling your important life purpose, rather than being required to use it repeatedly making money in order to feed your family and keep a roof over their heads. Ultimately, the goal with residual income is to *invest* your time to get money flowing rather than *spending* your time to get money that just needs to be earned again.

Of course there are genuine needs in every family for money, and trying to make your wants smaller only gets you so far. But just because you need to pay for certain needs doesn't mean you have to sacrifice all your time and even your dreams and life purpose in the pursuit of comforts and basic expenses.

Epictetus said, "Wealth consists not in having great possessions, but in having few wants."[5] It's true that avoiding uncontrolled spending and learning to say no to unnecessary things is an important part of financial fitness, one that we'll get into more in later chapters. But the idea that wanting little is the *only* key to financial fitness is fundamentally flawed.

GREAT INCOME FACTOR #4: BIG DREAMS ARE THE ONLY DREAMS

You don't need to be afraid to dream big and expect much from life, but it will be necessary to find a way to fund it all. In order to avoid letting your life purpose suffer for the sake of income, finding a pipeline income and connecting to your purpose itself is often the best answer for most people.

This is a simple idea, yet for many people it is exactly what is holding them back from being able to fully live the life they yearn for. Looking for opportunities and finding ways to implement this principle at the very beginning of your life career and financial path is extremely important.

So long as you have to spend your hours to get your dollars, you will always struggle to have the time and freedom to pursue whatever you want to dedicate your life to achieving. Well-planned residual income makes it possible for you to have both the time and money necessary to make your life about something other than the pursuit of resources to pay today's bills.

> **So long as you have to spend your hours to get your dollars, you will always struggle to have the time and freedom to pursue whatever you want to dedicate your life to achieving.**

For example, in the Marvel film *The Avengers*,[6] Captain

America asks Tony Stark (Iron Man) in a heated moment what he is without his suit of armor. Stark is quick on the uptake with his characteristically self-absorbed and self-congratulatory tone: "Uh, genius, billionaire, playboy, philanthropist." In other words, he's good how he is with or without the special suit. At this point, Captain America is thoroughly hushed, and Black Widow nods in agreement.

This is a guy who knows who he is: successful in various aspects of life because he had the time, resources, and freedom (consequences of business ownership and residual income) to pursue excellence in the things that mattered to him.

However, we don't bring this up to laud the fame of Iron Man or what he sees as his highest achievements. In fact, his response with the list of titles he could go by if not "Iron Man" reminds us of another guy, this one from history, who has an even more impressive list and a background to make it that much cooler.

TWO LOAVES OF BREAD

Consider the guy who, if he wasn't wearing his Founding Father suit, could have been called Printer, Humorist, Philanthropist, Inventor, Diplomat, Cartographer, Mentor, Abolitionist, or any of various other cool titles.

American hero Benjamin Franklin left home as a young teenager with very little to his name. When he started his career as a printer's apprentice, owning nothing but two loaves of bread, he was far from the man who later signed every American founding document, discovered the connection between lightning and electricity, invented the Franklin stove, pioneered American franchising, became the world's greatest diplomat, and ultimately changed the world in countless other ways.

> **If he wasn't wearing his Founding Father suit, Benjamin Franklin could have been called Printer, Humorist, Philanthropist, Inventor, Diplomat, Cartographer, Mentor, Abolitionist, or any of various other cool titles.**

Though, unlike the fictional Tony Stark, Franklin started from humble beginnings, he achieved incredible things—enough to warrant a place in history dozens of times over—because he understood the principles of greatness, including the difference between *good* ways to make money and *great* ones.

By leveraging his time and work in such a way that he could continue to draw income from his businesses long after investing the hours to start them up, he was able to free himself from the rut of having to work every day for every dollar and instead move the world toward his dream of what it should be. That's utilizing the power of residual income!

He is a powerful example and a great role model for you in these ways because he capitalized on his youth and his ability to *choose* the life he wanted to live and then worked hard and smart to build the kind of future he desired.

> **Use the place you're in, no matter how humble your present circumstances, to teach you the lessons that will make you excellent at whatever's next.**

He was also a good example of using the place you're in, no matter how humble your present circumstances, to teach you the lessons that will make you excellent at whatever's next and of constantly looking toward your bigger vision of success and contribution in life.

And of course, he never could have done even half of what he did if he hadn't had the kind of time and money that came from owning a business that connected with his purpose and brought him residual income. He dreamed big, and he did big things.

You want to be successful and change the world by living your unique life purpose. (That's why you're reading this book!) For that reason, we highly recommend that you study the life and teachings of Benjamin Franklin in further depth. While he wasn't perfect, he was a man who, in many ways, exemplified the kind of hero who starts the process of learning and applying the principles of financial fitness in his teens and ends up changing the world.

SILENT NODDING

As you set out on life's journey, remember the stories of Benjamin Franklin and others like him who were able to accomplish great things in the world and in their own lives by understanding and applying the right principles of financial fitness—especially when it came time to make an income.

Bad income is bad, and good income is better, but *great* income is the real goal. Make a choice, and start planning now to combine your income with your life purpose, own your own business, build residual income, and dream big!

Like Franklin, you may have to start small and work your way to greater heights as you go along. The key is to know and remember where you're headed as you make choices about how to make money, understanding the difference between good ways to get money and great ways. Then you can work toward the kind of future situation that has Captain America stumped for a reply and Black Widow nodding in agreement.

As you make the little choices in the right direction and never forget where you're headed, you will get closer and closer to the kind of financial freedom and personal achievement that took Franklin from being the printer's apprentice with nothing but a loaf of bread under each arm to the man who literally changed the world in politics, education, diplomacy, publishing, science, entrepreneurship, and business leadership. These financial principles (including the four factors of great income listed above) are powerful, and they will make a huge difference in the kind of freedom and lifestyle you'll be able to enjoy in later years.

Learn from Franklin, take advantage of the knowledge you're receiving and the fact that you're getting it now, and start taking the right steps toward a future filled with purpose, meaning, and happiness!

What services and accomplishments do you want to have credited to your name twenty years from now? Remember the financial fitness principles that actually work, start using and applying them, and you'll make *you* who you truly want to be!

The Four Factors of Great Income

1. There are bad ways to make money and good ways. Don't ever sacrifice morals or ethics for money. Be honest and live with integrity and character.
2. There are good ways to make money and great ways. Seeking great ways is best because it allows you to more fully live your dreams and serve others and enables you to fulfill your life purpose and improve the world.
3. The most important distinction between "good" income and "great" income is the attachment of income to your life purpose. Know your purpose, find a way to capitalize on it, and make enough money to always fully live it.
4. Business ownership is better than employment in the achievement of most purposes because it tends to allow more time and freedom to pursue a meaningful life path. Work toward ownership, and start looking for and using the opportunities and lessons that will get you there as early as possible.
5. Residual pipeline income is a better option than a cash-for-time scenario that only pays you once. Look for ways to build residual income, preferably in your own business. (The jobs you do now can

help teach you important lessons as you move in this direction.)

6. Follow good examples, and start now to build the kind of financial habits that will enable you to fully live your purpose, achieve the things you were born to do, and leave a meaningful legacy to the world around you.

7. Dream big! Then do the hard work to make your big dreams a reality, step by step.

GOING DEEPER
PART I

FOUR WAYS TO MAKE MONEY

In his book *Cashflow Quadrant*,[1] Robert Kiyosaki teaches that there are four basic ways to make money, each of which has different governing principles and concepts, along with its own set of pros and cons.

The four ways are as follows:

1. **Employee.** Most people understand this moneymaking method because the majority of people adopt this approach. Whether they work at the "top of the heap" or the very bottom, employees are those who have a job working *for* someone, or some company, to make their living. Kiyosaki points out that they are often driven by fear of economic uncertainty to seek security and benefits, which leads them to

sacrifice some independence and freedom and frequently settle for lower levels of income.

People in this group are usually dependent on their employer for their income, which means they are, to a certain extent, at the boss's beck and call in how they run their lives.

Employees may have less responsibility and hassle when it comes to dealing with factors like regulation, customer satisfaction, and many other big aspects of making a business successful. They also carry less of the risk that comes with stepping out on a limb and building something from square one. But these perks generally come with significantly reduced personal freedom, time, and money.

In fact, while many seek the employee situation to avoid risk or counter fear of economic downturn, it is important to note that *every* type of moneymaking method comes with its own set of risks and uncertainties. As we said, employees are frequently dependent on their employers for their living, which is a significant risk in itself. Not only can they be dragged into work in the middle of the night or on weekends or holidays, according to the boss's whims or the firm's needs, but they can also be transferred, demoted, or even fired or laid off (as a result of the economic crises they so often fear).

2. **Self-Employed.** This method of earning income often includes people who look for security in personal independence. By throwing off employment and becoming their own boss, they hope to achieve real prosperity and security in doing things themselves.

    This group is characterized by its sense of independence and personal competence. Self-employed people often know they're good—the best—and they choose to let their success and financial well-being rise and fall on their own merits and hard work. The motto of the self-employed is often something along this line: "If you want something done right, do it yourself."

    Because they're naturally independent, self-employed people often have more control over their lives than employees—like when they get to vacation, what hours they work, and how many sick days they can take in a year. Unfortunately, as many find out too late, this is only true if they are able to get their business to a place where they can afford to take *any* vacations, hours off work, or sick days at all.

For some, being self-employed means more money, more time, and more freedom, but in many cases, it can mean a lot of extra hours at the office and quite a bit of added stress. To put it simply, when you're self-employed, you are "the man." If you aren't making your income happen, it's not happening.

The major con shared by both employees and the self-employed is that they are by nature *active* forms of income, meaning that they require you to continuously and consistently work in order to have any sort of paycheck coming in.

An employee trades his or her time for money. This can either be fair or unfair, but either way, it has a major drawback: You can have either time *or* money—seldom both. When you've got a lot of one, you frequently don't have enough of the other.

The same is usually true of the self-employed, at least at first. In both of these two groups, you have to be there putting in hours of work, or you won't make an income.

Interestingly, while these first two groups make up most of the population of the United States (and other nations), they account for only a very small portion of the wealth!

Because of these significant downsides, Kiyosaki says the goal for those who want financial success is to get to the "other side of the quadrant"—to achieve a residual form of income through the third or fourth method of earning income.

3. **Business Owner.** Unlike self-employed people, who are usually focused on doing things themselves and being *independent*, business owners are about building systems and teams that will generate income and being *interdependent*. These incomes are generally ongoing or what we might call "residual."

Business owners learn to delegate tasks and build teams of people who *together* can do things better than the owners ever could on their own.

By investing time and work at the beginning to create a system (or investing capital to purchase one) that doesn't rely on their presence and hours of personal hard work to continue functioning, business owners are building a "pipeline" of residual income.

Once the pipeline is built, they can spend their time working on their life purpose and increasing the business success of all involved (or going on a month-long trip to Italy, for that matter) and continue to make good, consistent income. This way, they have time and money in abundance and are able to devote themselves to what they genuinely care about rather than being tied down in swapping hours for money.

While significant risk and hard work are certainly involved in building and maintaining this type of financial situation, the freedom and prosperity it offers are clearly worth it!

4. **Investor.** Kiyosaki explains that in order to qualify for this group, you have to have enough money that you could realistically *lose* $250,000 on a failed investment without considering it a serious setback. Having met that financial requirement, it's all about financial wisdom and compound interest.

    Successful investors make their money by having money and knowing how to put it in places that will increase it exponentially. Nearly all investors start out by becoming successful business owners first, as the lessons of ownership are essential knowledge for becoming effective investors.

    Kiyosaki says that to become truly *wealthy*, a person needs to reach this level of income. But the focus of many such investors is to continue to invest in their own business, tied as it is to their life purpose, rather than risk their hard-earned resources on outside investments.

This is different than how investors are often portrayed on television or in the media, but it is more in keeping with a life of financial fitness and serving others to help improve society.

These last two groups (business owners and investors) make up a very small percentage of the population, and guess how much of the wealth they have? That's right! The bulk of it.

As an interesting side note, successful author and entrepreneur Grant Cardone says the number-one reason business owners and investors have so much of the wealth is that they read an average of more than sixty books a year, while most of the population reads on average less than one.

SAVING MONEY

PERCENTAGE POWER!

*Save a part of your income and begin now, for the man
with a surplus controls circumstances and the man
without a surplus is controlled by circumstances.*
—HENRY H. BUCKLEY

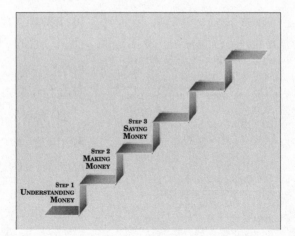

Having established the right mindset for viewing and
making money, perhaps the primary thing for you to
learn about finances is to save, save, save.

In most cases, as a teen, you have very few set expenses, so now is the best time to establish the proper savings habits, before the temptation *not* to save becomes a huge factor in your decision-making process.

Waiting to start saving until you have hungry kids and a stack of bills to pay is a bad idea, and waiting to establish the *habit* of saving will make your work many, many times harder. As Joe Moore said, "A simple fact that is hard to learn is that the time to save money is when you have some."

If you don't start saving money right now, every time you bring some in, making the commitment and establishing the habit, no matter what other things are calling for your pennies, you will likely never start. This means you'll never

---

Example of Percentages for Child/Youth Income*

- 25% life savings
- 25% emergency savings
- 10% tithing
- 10% charity, offerings, and miscellaneous giving
- 15% targeted purchase savings or additional savings
- 15% fun/free use or additional savings

We'll get into each of these in more depth as each item comes along, but studying this chart and referring to it often will help you understand and learn the big picture of how your money should flow for the best results and optimal financial fitness.

*Note that the recommended percentages for children and youth are different than those for adults. (The adult recommendations are outlined in *Financial Fitness: The Offense, Defense and Playing Field of Personal Finance*.[1]) Also, there is nothing scientific about these numbers, but rather they are to be used as guidelines. The important thing is to determine an arrangement similar to this that works for you and then stick to it.

stop desperately needing the results of having started twenty years ago.

Are you sensing the theme? You can't start too soon, and putting it off will never get it done.

CONTROL YOUR CONTROL

The Henry Buckley quote that opens this chapter teaches this point very well and shows why the principle of saving is so important. Frankly, the only time you really have to control is right now. The only money you have to control is the cash you have in your hands right now.

But when you use the control you have in *this* moment with *this* cash to plan and prepare for *future* circumstances of varying types and degrees, you are using the stewardship of the *now* to extend your scope and influence in future events, challenges, and opportunities.

And how do you increase your power and security in this way? Take a piece of everything you get in the "now" and save it for the "what ifs," the "whens," and the "if onlys."

> **Take a piece of everything you get in the "now" and save it for the "what ifs," the "whens," and the "if onlys."**

We promise you this: there will be times (lots of them) when you want more money than you'd normally have on hand, either to deal with some unforeseen difficulty or

emergency expense or to take advantage of some opportunity or investment.

If you commit now and consistently save a piece of
everything you ever make, you will be much better
prepared to approach such situations with a smile
and an open checkbook—rather than a fight with your
spouse, an hour of tears on the couch, and another huge
credit card debt that will never look smaller again or at
best, a missed opportunity for growth, fun, or impact in
your life purpose.

Low Expenses Shouldn't Mean Adding Artificial Ones

As we mentioned earlier, right now you generally
have significantly fewer and smaller set expenses than
adults do, since you probably don't have a house (with
a mortgage, utilities, taxes, or flooded bathrooms), kids
(with braces, sports teams, music lessons, or never-
ending appetites), or mountains of student loans, car
payments, and the like.

The point is while you often make less than an adult,
you almost always have fewer demands on what you *do*
make. This is a blessing for those who learn to save and
prepare for future expenses. Unfortunately, however,
often the lack of a real demand leads to the creation of
an artificial one. Since you don't have creditors calling
you or banging down your door to get you to pay your
bills, it's easy to feel that the demands of this or that toy
are just as great as if the power were shut off.

Sometimes the fact that you don't have to pay off a card leads to the mentality of "I *have* to make this purchase" or "I *have* to have that music download, leather bag, or newest game."

Using money you do have to buy things you want isn't always bad, but replacing the genuine demands of real expenses with a made-up sense of need is not in keeping with financial fitness. It's vitally important to financial success that such purchases and expenses, in general, take their proper place in the list of priorities.

In reality, this is just as true for adults' mortgage payments as it is for a new Xbox, but the difference in actual demand makes it a lot easier for you to start thinking of savings in the right way because you aren't going to lose a house if you deny yourself the Xbox. And, in fairness, while it still needs to have its proper place in our priorities, the mortgage tends to have a higher natural place than the Xbox (as it should).

In any event, the principle is simple and pivotal to success: save, save, save! Start now, be consistent, and do this *before* you rush to the store to get that new pair of shoes.

Teens who want to be truly successful should adopt the mindset that says, "The fact

> **Adopt the mindset that says, "The fact that I have small expenses doesn't mean I have more to spend; it means I have more to *save*."**

that I have small expenses doesn't mean I have more to spend; it means I have more to *save*."

What Do You *Keep*?

The first principle of financial fitness taught in the book *Financial Fitness* from the LIFE Leadership Essentials Series states, "It's not what you make but what you keep that determines financial success. Pay yourself first and save what you pay yourself."[2]

When it comes to the things you actually *do* to be financially successful, this is step number one. We've talked a lot already about the right financial mindset, the significance of your life purpose, and the power of business ownership and residual income. Now we get to the specific details of what to do with your everyday finances. This is extremely important!

So you just got home from work and are holding your first paycheck (or the seventh or the thousandth or whichever one it is for you). The first thing to do is to take a predetermined percentage out of it and put it straight in the bank to save for your future. Then you're going to *leave it there!*

This is how savings works! And it really does work. If you want to be financially fit, being a saver is essential. As a young person, develop the habit of saving. This one practice will have a huge, positive

> **If you want to be financially fit, being a saver is essential.**

influence on your financial fitness for the rest of your life.

For example, in 2010, the story of a young girl who understood the power of savings went big in Ohio media and even bigger on the Internet.

This farm girl had been involved with her local county fairs and 4-H program showing hogs year after year from the time she was four years old, when she won—and saved—her first $100. According to news articles, she spent part of her earnings for the first time on a purse when she was fourteen years old.

Years went by, and she continued her showing, winning, and saving, until she made her second purchase at age eighteen, when she bought a four-bed-room, two-bathroom house, paying with cash.

While it might not be your goal to buy a house with cash when you're eighteen, you can probably recognize that being *able* to do so is a pretty good financial situation compared to where most people are at that stage of life, and the $40,000 cash she spent on the property would probably be helpful in accomplishing whatever your goal *is*. Or you could just keep it in your savings account.

But the story doesn't end there. She continued to live with her parents through college and rented the house to others, still saving all her profits for the future.

While the idea of saving for the future without knowing exactly what that means might seem pointless to some, since "the future" is a vague idea that doesn't appear as important as some of the things you could be spending money on in the present, it is actually extremely important. It is vital to financial fitness. The level of your savings is a clear indication of how financially fit you actually are.

Some teens may know exactly what future dreams and goals they're saving for, while others might just feel that they will need/want their savings for *something*. Either way, saving now will open all sorts of doors for you in the future and keep a bunch of others from slamming shut in your face—or on your fingers or toes.

> **Saving now will open all sorts of doors for you in the future and keep a bunch of others from slamming shut in your face— or on your fingers or toes.**

Financially fit people don't just save in order to spend their money later. They save because of the powerful options it gives them in the future. It is also, quite plainly, the right thing to do.

MAKING SENSE OF PERCENTAGES

In this example, the Ohio girl saved 100 percent of her income, with the exception of one small purchase at the age of fourteen. We're not saying this is necessary. In fact, there are a few other things we recommend giving a consistent percentage of your income to, so don't get too carried away. That said, assuming you also budget for those other things, which we'll talk about in the next few chapters, saving as much as you can from an early age is a great idea!

Of course, we do have some recommendations for what percentages to use. You should have a specific commitment that you never under any circumstances drop below. To repeat: Pick a percentage, and always save that much from everything you earn. The

> **Pick a percentage, and always save that much from everything you earn.**

percentage should be at least 20 percent, but we recommend higher.

It's okay to dedicate a larger amount than your regular plan to savings whenever you want, but it's extremely important that you don't allow this to lead you to do less than usual on other income. There should be an exact percentage—agreed on with the help of parents and financial mentors—that you save every time you get money, no matter what. After that, you can save more when you feel like it, *but never less*. Ever!

As far as what that number should be, successful business leader Orrin Woodward says that any time his children make money—whether it's 30¢ or $3,000—50 percent goes directly to savings. So when they want to buy something that costs $10, they know they need to make at least $20. Period.

Fifty percent is what we recommend for most teens, but you should work it out with your parents and mentors.

That said, as a rule, your set percentage should be no lower than 20 percent. This is so important that we'll mention it over and over. And again, this is the savings account that only gets deposits—not withdrawals. You are paying yourself and building your future.

Half of what you are saving is actually for future opportunities and emergencies, and the rest is meant specifically for building your overall wealth. You may even want to create two separate accounts to track the different types of savings.

For the wealth-building part of your savings (we'll call it Life Savings), there may come a time—a long time from now and with lots of mentoring—when it's right to change the medium of your investment into some-thing other than deposited bank money (like a house to rent, gold, and so on). But you should be able to track the money you put in this account as the amount you're worth, and it should never shrink for the rest of your life.

It's actually really fun to build this account as you go about your business, knowing that, all things being equal, you'll never be poorer than you are today, ever again.

There are other types of savings that can be an important aspect of your financial approach, but we'll get into that in a moment. For now, we're talking about the long-term savings that represent your future capital and, in essence, the financial legacy you'll leave to your children and grandchildren.

You are not too young to think about this. In fact, the younger you are, the better! Saving is an essential habit of financial fitness and money success, and it's time for you to get good at it!

So to recap, put 50 percent or more (certainly not less than 20 percent) of everything you make into savings—half as long-term Life Savings you'll never spend and the other half as an emergency fund. Start doing this right now, and never stop.

You should be in the habit of never touching the emergency fund part of your savings for any reason (outside of absolute, dire emergencies). Handle it the way you do your Life Savings, and you'll be much better prepared to deal with the real emergencies and financial issues that arise later in life—times when you'll actually *need* it.

In any event, you should never even dip into this account without being specifically counseled by your parents and financial mentors to do so—and then *only* as they counsel.

This may seem harsh, but you will be *so* glad you made and stuck to this commitment in the long run. And if you need more money for other things, find creative ways to *make* more money. Part of financial fitness is the creativity, innovation, and hard work of procuring what you need.

SAVING *FOR* SOMETHING

Another essential part of financial fitness is saving for things you wouldn't be able to afford on the percentage of an individual paycheck you have set aside for personal spending. Rather than using debt or robbing the other important priorities in your life, you can set aside a percentage of your income over a period of time for making a particular purchase in the future. This is in addition to the amount you're already saving (as described in the section above).

> **Rather than using debt or robbing the other important priorities in your life, you can set aside a percentage of your income over a period of time for making a particular purchase in the future.**

For example, sixteen-year-old Jake *really* wanted the mountain bike he had seen advertised at the department store last week. His old one was okay, but it was well worn, and he had big plans for biking this summer.

The one at the store was really something! Not to mention, it came at a great price. But no matter how he stretched his "fun money," the $50 he had simply wouldn't buy a $200 bike. There was no getting around that.

He knew he couldn't use his savings for a purchase like this, and taking away from tithing to get a new bike was *never* a good idea. Jake understood by now—yes, he'd learned this the hard way, unfortunately—that the moment when money seems short is the *worst* time to start cheating on the rules of financial fitness.

> **The moment when money seems short is the *worst* time to start cheating on the rules of financial fitness.**

Still, he really wanted the bike, and it was a fantastic deal! But, as Jake was fond of reminding himself at such times, you can totally recognize the value of something to be a million dollars, but if you don't have the money, you won't buy it—even though you know it's worth it.

OWN YOUR BIKE

Of course, he knew that if he could find a way to get the money without any debt, that would be the best route. While others might have been fine with any old way of earning the cash, Jake preferred only *good* options. He wasn't going to become some sort of indentured servant for the bike, and that included debt in his mind. It's hard to get a lot of biking in when someone else owns your very existence. Plus, he wanted the bike to be *his,* not the other way around.

That meant more creativity than following the *store's* idea of using debt as a solution to insufficient funds.

He thought about it for a minute and realized he was a bit out of his league. *Time to bring out the big guns,* he said to himself, and then he went seeking a good financial mentor. He walked into the kitchen where his mom was just starting dinner.

"Hey, can I help with the salad? I need some money advice."

She smiled and nodded. "You know the drill," she replied.

Jake explained the situation while he got out the salad stuff and got to work.

Mom listened and waited patiently until he finished before asking, "Are you sure you should be getting this bike at all?"

They discussed the topic for a while until Mom and Jake were agreed that the bike wasn't a bad purchase—as long as it fit his budget in other ways. It would actually help him in more ways than just fun. He'd be working at some scout camps with his dad over the summer, and having a decent mountain bike would make the whole experience easier and better. He'd be better at his job.

Once they'd answered that question, Mom had a few others. "Do you have any big goals you need more motivation on right now?"

"Well, I've been meaning to de-junk my desk area and, in fact, my whole room. I don't seem to have enough room for my growing book collection—all the boxes of trading cards and various electronics are getting in the way."

"Great," said Mom. "I think you can connect all of these issues in a way that brings fantastic results. Do you want to hear about it?"

"That's what I'm here for!"

Using *What* You Want to Become *Who* You Want

"Okay. First, I recommend setting aside half of your fun money every month to save up for the bike. Since your fun money is 30 percent of your income, that's 15 percent of your earnings each month. That'll be a sacrifice for the next few months, but it'll get you to the bike, and you'll still have the other 15 percent."

"Yeah, but I'm going to want it in June, for sure, and that's only five months away. Don't I need a higher percentage?" Jake asked.

"That's where the de-junking comes in. Any thoughts?"

Jake considered for a minute. This was the cool thing about going to Mom for mentoring: She always made him come up with his own answers. In some ways, it seemed like he may as well have stayed in his room, since he was still just asking himself questions, but being with Mom and following her targeted questions made all the difference. It always did.

That was when it hit him. If junk he wasn't using and didn't need was getting in the way of things he did care about, and he also had a fund deficiency, perhaps a yard sale was in order.

He excitedly mentioned it to Mom and went on for a minute before he realized his desk full of games wouldn't make much of a yard sale, even if he threw in his old bike and the two boxes of stuff he had in the garage. He was starting to get discouraged when he noticed Mom listening to his rambling.

"Hey, wait! Do you have anything you could throw in, just to make it look better and bigger? I've heard you and Dad talking about doing one. Can I sell some stuff too?"

"Since you're here proactively and responsibly looking for solutions (instead of just asking me to get you the bike), I'll do you one better. We do have a bunch of used furniture, kids' clothes, and random household items that we'd be thrilled to part with, but we really don't want to plan and run a yard sale right now.

"So get your room in a state that makes you happy and clears the way for your books and new bike. On top of that, I'll give you a list of things we want sold, and if you do all the work cleaning the garage and house, moving stuff, setting up signs, planning, and running the yard sale, we'll split the proceeds with you 50/50. That's on our stuff, of course. You'll get 100 percent on anything that was yours to begin with. What do you think?"

That sounded great, any way Jake sliced it! It would take some work, but it would get him that bike! Not to mention, he really wanted to increase his bedroom shelf space anyway.

Finishing the salad, he told his mom he'd accept the challenge and went to call his older sister about running a successful yard sale; he didn't want to fail simply out of procrastination. He also canceled all his plans for watching TV for the next five months so he'd have a lot more time to work and to read his books.

He worked hard over the next five months and said no to a few chances to spend more than his 15 percent. In the end, he'd improved his life in several ways. For one, he had the bike he wanted without compromising on the commitments he'd made to himself about his financial fitness.

On top of that, his room was full of books instead of his old games, and the yard sale had been a big hit! He'd even made a little more than he needed for the bike and was able to add more titles to his overflowing bookshelves—not to mention the great experience and wisdom he'd gained making the yard sale a success. He was learning a ton and biking a lot too! It was going to be a great summer!

Illustrations and Introductions

This story illustrates how you can use the power of saving a little bit consistently over time to get something specific you want but wouldn't be able to afford with your spending money from just one paycheck. The power of savings is amazing.

It also introduces another powerful financial fitness principle: use the things you want to *have* to help motivate you to do the things you want to *accomplish*. Setting a life goal along with your financial

> **Use the things you want to *have* to help motivate you to do the things you want to *accomplish*.**

ones and making it a requirement for extra purchases

is a powerful way to keep expenses in check and accomplish a lot more in life. It's also a good way to capitalize on the power of want.

Even if his mom hadn't suggested going halves in the yard sale, Jake was in the right creative mindset to come up with a solution to his financial concern. It might have taken longer, or he might have thought of a job or project that paid even more. Also, the fact that he didn't just ask his mom for money showed that he was trying to come up with a good solution himself—not just seeking a handout.

By the way, take note of how important it is to consult with mentors in all this. Not only did Jake's mom ask the right questions and help him stick to his commitments, but she was also able to help him see more of the available solutions and even offer up some that he couldn't have enjoyed without her assistance.

This is often the power of mentoring, so don't think you're better off on your own! The added support, perspective, and problem solving is not a small thing. In fact, it's huge! To say it simply, learn good principles and listen to good mentors—and then use them! This truly does work, and it might just be the *only* thing that does.

THREE KINDS OF SAVINGS

So far, we've discussed three kinds of savings, and all are very important. These include the following:

1. Life Savings

This is your wealth, money you'll always save. As you continue to save, this fund will keep growing bigger and bigger for the rest of your life. It never shrinks!

As you continue to save and accumulate wealth in this way, you will be preparing and developing a fantastic legacy to leave to your family or to a cause that matters deeply to you.

We've already talked about Benjamin Franklin and how he has lots to teach us about financial fitness. There's another, less well-known story about Franklin that teaches some of the power of long-term savings and the impact it can make on the world, particularly in the realm of finances.

After living a financially fit life, building several successful businesses and making long-term savings a priority, Franklin was able to leave £1,000 each in trust to the cities of Boston and Philadelphia. In US currency, that amount was worth over $4,000 in his time, which amounts to over $100,000 in ours.

Having such savings available to leave to something that matters to you is pretty cool in the first place and shows why long-term savings are so important. And of course, since he stipulated in his will that the funds weren't to be touched for two hundred years, the story does an even better job of expressing the point.

As the money sat in savings, not being used or spent for two centuries, it built huge amounts of interest and ended up being a fund of several million dollars, which was used to build important foundations, help the communities in meaningful ways, and fund other projects that could never have happened without the long-term thinking, vision, and legacy of Benjamin Franklin.

Whatever your long-term savings end up meaning to your posterity or to the world, know that living this principle will be a small sacrifice you make on a consistent basis now that has the power to create an enormous difference in the future. Your Life Savings will be a powerful legacy in whatever way makes sense for your life purpose.

2. Emergency Savings

This savings is for real emergencies when you are older. We can't stress enough how valuable this fund will be to you when you really need it. No matter what comes up and gives you the right reason to use these funds, trust us; you'll be glad you have the money available.

It's hard to imagine or plan for the specific financial needs and crises that will come along during your journey, but, luckily, you don't have to. The specifics don't matter much right now. It's enough to know that someday you will be able to use this money. And if Murphy's Law holds true, you'll feel like you need it even more if you don't have it. So make it a priority!

Think of any people you've known who have had a financial emergency. Consider the pain it caused and the ways it bled into and impacted every other aspect of life, far beyond finances. Would it have made a difference if they'd started saving 25 percent—or even 10 percent—of everything they made back when they were your age?

We don't mean to pick on them, not at all. We are merely hoping you'll be able to learn from their experience and understand how much this matters—how much power you have to make a different decision and choose a different outcome.

Sometimes this might seem hard or worthless, but as you remember the people who have found themselves in financial emergencies *without* this preparation, or even speak with them about it, it will become clear to you that the little you're giving up now will be completely worth it when the time comes for you to draw on the wisdom and self-discipline of today that will turn into real money in the future.

Here's the bottom line: Even if you never end up needing or wanting your Emergency Savings for important things in your own future, the worst-case scenario will be that you're left with a bunch of extra wealth. You have nothing to lose, except a few

> **You have nothing to lose, except a few extra dollars' worth of present gratification, and it will be more than worth it in your future.**

extra dollars' worth of present gratification, and it will be more than worth it in your future.

3. Targeted Savings

You'll use your Targeted Savings for a special future purchase. This is where the principle of delayed gratification comes into full force, and it's what Jake did to get his mountain bike.

There are things you want that you can't afford right now because they cost a lot or because you're dedicated to financial fitness, and the percentage of your income you use for personal spending isn't big enough.

Delayed gratification is putting off the purchase of such things until you have a financially fit way to pay for them, rather than betraying your financial fitness by spending more than the set-aside percentage, using debt, or making some other type of financially unfit choice to try to buffer the money you have for such expenses.

Delayed gratification is an extremely important and powerful tool of financial fitness. As you commit to living these principles and refuse to cheat yourself in any way, delaying your gratification and using the power of savings to get the things you want in a way and at a time when you can afford them, you will see big results and a life full of abundance and real happiness.

You have the power in this, and saving up is far better than getting what you want when you can't or shouldn't afford it. Developing the habit of delayed gratification and saving for what you want will help you stay out of financial bondage, and such discipline will teach you the skills and lessons you need to be successful in other aspects of life as well. It will also help you build your bank accounts into solid financial reservoirs.

Learning this lesson and using these tools will help you make your future *yours*, instead of leading you to find your future self a slave to past mistakes, debts, or lack of funds.

Hard work, delayed gratification, and creativity are vital characteristics of financially fit people and great leaders.

Start Now and Get Going!

The power of saving—whether it's for life wealth accumulation, a rainy-day emergency fund, or a specific targeted purchase—is absolutely incredible! The way it will push you to be creative, resourceful, and driven toward your mission is extremely valuable for your personal development. Beyond that, the difference it will make in your ability to meet the future challenges and opportunities that await you will be truly priceless.

So start saving! Remember, the time to save money is when you *have* money, not when you *need* it. Indeed, the time is *right now*—and *every* time you get any income. Don't put it off for another paycheck or a better month. Start with whatever you have in front of you today and then tomorrow and then the day after that. Set a strict percentage (at least 20 percent, preferably more), and stick to it no matter what. Communicate this percentage with your parents, and let them help you stick to the plan.

Use the power of saving to help you accomplish goals and get the things you want to have. Develop these habits now! It will only get harder as you get older and your responsibilities increase and multiply. But the earlier you start, the easier it will be to form good habits that will last a lifetime.

In addition, as you truly apply and live these principles, your financial and leadership results will amaze you. This one choice, leveraging the power of percentages by learning the recommended savings percentages and committing to following them with all your income, will give you great options later on in your life. So start now!

STEP 3 SUMMARY

Save Preset Percentages of All Your Income

1. Save, save, save!
2. Financially fit people don't just save now to spend later. They save because saving is the right thing to do.
3. Start saving a specific percentage (preferably 50 percent or more, but not less than 20 percent) of everything you make, and do it *right now*! Never dip below your percentage for any reason.
4. Leave your savings alone! Some of it is for personal wealth accumulation, and the rest is for your future. Either way, put it away immediately, and do not touch it.
5. Save in all three major ways:
    a) Life Savings that you never spend (10–25 percent or more of all your income)
    b) Emergency Savings (10–25 percent or more of all your income)
    c) Targeted Savings
6. Hard work, delayed gratification, and creativity are vital characteristics of financially fit people and great leaders.
7. Never stop saving a percentage of your income for future needs and opportunities. Even if there comes a time to invest in some other medium (like starting your own business or, like the Ohio girl

mentioned earlier, using part of your savings to buy a rental house that brings you income instead of leaving it all in the bank), you can never have too much savings.

8. If you need to spend more than you have left over, creatively come up with ways to *make* more.

9. Develop the habit of saving up for things you want, rather than cheating on the principles of financial fitness or dipping in to your Life or Emergency Savings. It's much better to wait a few weeks, months, or even years for what you want than to get yourself into financial trouble by failing to apply the principles and techniques of real financial fitness. The percentages have power, if you use them!

10. Even when you can afford more, save your "fun" purchases and use them as rewards for accomplishing your goals in life.

11. We can't say it enough: always counsel with and listen to the right financial mentors!

GIVING MONEY

SMILE BIG ☺

You make a living by what you get;
you make a life by what you give.

—UNKNOWN, OFTEN ATTRIBUTED TO WINSTON CHURCHILL

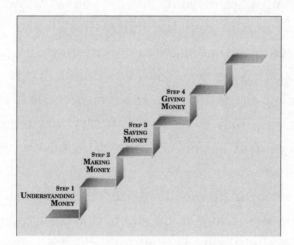

Giving is an aspect of financial fitness that goes hand in hand with saving, and it is second in this book only because they couldn't both be first. In reality, you prepare to give at the same time you take out your percentages for savings, and it is every bit as important. You don't ever want to skip or fudge this step.

When you recognize the money in your life as both a blessing and a responsibility, the need to give to others is clear. No matter how much or how little you make, you should always set aside a percentage to give away to others.

> **No matter how much or how little you make, you should always set aside a percentage to give away to others.**

As you do, even when you're struggling and it seems hard to give up part of your "little," you will find a spirit of abundance in your life that will help you feel truly happy, despite challenges and hard times.

In fact, giving when it's hard often helps you, the giver, even more than the receiver because it takes the focus away from your own difficulty and leads you to center your attention on those who have even bigger problems.

Well-known financial adviser Suze Orman teaches that the first thing to do when you realize you are in a financial difficulty is to write a check to charity. This helps you realize that a lot of people are far worse off than you.

Oftentimes your financial difficulties as a young person are relatively small compared to those faced by many adults. The percentage of your income dedicated to giving may seem small to you as well, but you'd be surprised how far a little bit goes when a person has a desperate need. A little bit is a really big deal when you have nothing at all.

When your own challenges seem hardest, consider that there is always someone worse off than you, which puts you in a position to make a huge difference in somebody else's life. Giving can turn times of worry and stress into service opportunities and powerful moments of growth and contribution.

> **Giving can turn times of worry and stress into service opportunities and powerful moments of growth and contribution.**

At the same time you hold your brand-new paycheck and take out 20–50 percent or more for savings, you should take an additional 10 percent for tithing and a little more for other offerings. There are lots of good charities and causes out there that could use your help, no matter how small. Do some research to find one or a few that have meaning to you, and start giving today!

CRY FOR *THEM* INSTEAD

Sam and Leah sat looking at their bank statements again. It had been like this every month this year. Leah hadn't started crying yet, but it was only a matter of time.

Jane, their seventeen-year-old, desperately needed braces. It was one of those times when it wasn't just about cosmetics or beauty. Jane's jaw alignment was off in such a way that it pulled her neck out and left her in constant pain, which the chiropractor said would lead to serious injury and permanent damage if it wasn't handled ASAP.

But that wasn't the whole story, not even close. They had been struggling to make ends meet for months, and this expense was just too big to fit in. They had been saving every penny. They were wearing worn-out clothes from who knew when, they had no TV and had to go to the library for Internet needs, and they hadn't been on a date in forever—which they told themselves was fine, since they didn't have time for that even if they *could* afford it.

Every moment home from work, Sam spent trying to build their business and make it a sustainable source of income, but it was still just beginning and required a lot of time.

In short, they had cut expenses in every way they could imagine, and still the bills always seemed bigger than the paychecks. They had been faithfully giving to savings each month, as their financial mentor had taught them. But they still couldn't seem to get out of the hole, and they wouldn't rob those accounts for normal expenses.

They might consider taking from their emergency fund for the braces, depending on what their mentor thought would be best. But even with that, there wasn't enough to fully pay for them, and Sam still had to find a way to get halfway across the country in two months for business training.

Thinking about all this, Leah finally started to cry. She hated crying—it always made Sam feel like a failure—but sometimes it was all too much. Sam held her for a few minutes as she wept. *What could they possibly do?*

As they sat and worried about everything that seemed to be pressing down on them, it occurred to Sam that they had never handed in their tithing check or the small one they had written for charity from their previous paycheck.

They still had the checks on the fridge and the money in the account; they simply hadn't delivered them yet. Sam went and grabbed the checks and sat down again next to his wife. They looked at the checks for a moment, and Leah smiled through her tears. She grabbed a tissue and wiped her face. "There is someone out there, bawling on the couch, who needs this money right now," she stated. Sam gave her a big hug. Then they got in the car and went to deliver the checks.

This is a true story, which has happened in one way or another to hundreds of people throughout the world. Sometimes our challenges seem too big to handle, and our lot seems too hard.

Taking the opportunity to consider those we can serve and help in such situations and then giving even a little bit to make their lives easier and better can transform such moments from painful to powerful.

In this scenario, giving of what little Sam and Leah had didn't make the problems go away, but it *did* make them seem smaller and more manageable. It also gave the couple the chance to be unified in a cause that mattered to them, rather than merely focusing on their own problems. And they really did make a difference in the lives of others by giving of their meager substance. Like the story of the widow's pennies in the Bible,[1] giving when giving seemed impossible gave them great happiness.

Developing the habit of giving now, no matter how broke you are, will help you keep a clear perspective on your own challenges, and it is also an important part of fulfilling your responsibility as a steward over your money.

OTHER TYPES OF GIVING

> **Pay tithes and offerings *before* you spend all your money on other things, and give even when you have very little.**

That's about all we have to say about the specific percentages of financial giving that ought to be a part of your financial fitness regimen. Our main concern is to emphasize this important principle: pay tithes and offerings *before* you spend all your money on other things, and give even when you have very little.

This is vitally important to your financial success and will also have a huge impact on your overall happiness.

It's part of your money stewardship, so make it a priority. And start right now so it becomes a habit while you're still young. Be sure to pay tithes and offerings first thing, along with setting aside your savings percentages, whenever you make *any* money. Don't wait until later.

With that understood, let's talk about some other powerful and important types of giving that will also help you fulfill your stewardship of money and also bring a lot of happiness and satisfaction into your life.

Along with giving a specific percentage of your income, get into the habit of giving and serving in more than just monetary ways. As you seek to improve the world and the lives of those around you and make meaningful contributions to society through your own personal life purpose, you will find yourself to be much happier in general and also a lot better suited to accomplish your goals and aspirations in life.

> **Obtaining money doesn't necessarily make you happy or "successful." Serving, loving, and helping others using your unique gifts and talents, however, naturally brings more happiness and fulfillment.**

As we've said earlier, seeking and obtaining money doesn't necessarily make you happy or "successful." Serving, loving, and helping others using your unique gifts and talents, however, naturally brings more happiness and fulfillment, which is the same thing as increased success.

So along with giving your money, look for ways to give your time and talents to those who will benefit from your help and service. Seek out chances to serve and lift those around you as a part of your money stewardship and your life purpose. As you do so, you will be a happier person and a better steward over all your gifts and blessings. This will make you more effective at everything you attempt, and it will help you keep the big picture, and your place in it, in focus as you strive to make the world a better place and yourself a better person.

> **Along with giving your money, look for ways to give your time and talents to those who will benefit from your help and service.**

SAM AND LEAH

When Sam and Leah dropped off the checks to their pastor and got back in the car to drive home, Sam began brainstorming ways to get the needed income for Jane's braces. He shared his ideas, and Leah excitedly joined in with him. She reached into her purse, pulled out a small notebook and pen, and started writing down their ideas.

As they waited at a stoplight, Leah realized she was smiling and turned to Sam. "I know we can figure this out. It will take some extra hard work, but we're going to get through this. With both of us working on it together, we'll make the extra money."

Her enthusiasm was infectious, and Sam nodded. "I have another idea," he said, and Leah positioned her pen to write one more potential solution in her notebook....

TONI'S LESSON

A week later, on the other side of town, Toni took her three children to a burger joint. It had been a long day, and she was exhausted. Her husband was away on business for a few days, and she had just finished an afternoon library trip with the kids.

They usually didn't go out for burgers, preferring to save the money, but tonight Toni was just too tired to go home and cook a meal.

When the waitress took their order, her six-year-old son Josh waited until everyone else had ordered. Cocking his head to one side in deep thought, he asked the waitress, "If I get the meal deal with the drink, I'll be saving an extra 89¢, right?"

Surprised, the waitress tried to do the math in her head.

Josh kept talking while she calculated. "Actually, if I just order the burger and fries but no drink at all, I'll save $1.19. That's 30¢ better than the full meal deal, which is 89¢ better than ordering them all separately." Josh smiled happily. "That's what I'll do. Please bring me that with no pop and just the free cup for ice water. Thank you."

Toni couldn't help but laugh at this, and her tiredness melted away for a moment. "You've really been listening to the financial principles your dad and I have been discussing, haven't you, Josh?"

The little boy smiled. "Yes. And I'm going to always be a big saver like you and Dad."

When her husband called to check in later that evening, Toni was excited to share Josh's story. "We all canceled our sodas and got ice water," she told him. "Of course, we could have afforded the pop. But Josh's enthusiasm for financial fitness was infectious, and we all wanted to join in the savings."

"That's great," her husband said. "These principles of financial fitness are so powerful. The day we started reading that book was a turning point in our lives."

Toni nodded while she laughed happily. "I never knew it could be this way," she replied. "I feel so blessed. Oh, and I haven't even told you the best part yet. When we got home, I gave Josh the $5.00 he earned for cleaning the whole garage like you asked him to, and he went to his room and spent an hour counting, planning, and making change from his piggy bank. Then he came back and handed me $2.50 for his savings and another 50¢ to save toward that new baseball bat he wants."

"Excellent," her husband said.

"But then he did something amazing. It brought tears to my eyes."

"What?"

"He handed me another $1.50 and said, 'Fifty cents is for tithing, and the rest is for the fund for Jane's braces. You know, Jane, the one who babysits us sometimes, and the jar someone put out in the foyer at church for her braces?'

"I was so touched that I told him what a good man he is growing up to be, and you know what he said next?"

"What?" Toni's husband asked, clearly touched by his son's actions.

"He said, 'Mom, if I'm giving 20 percent of my income this week to help Jane, and you and Dad give some of yours, too, she'll have braces in no time.'"

They both laughed.

"What did you tell him?" he asked.

"I told him I'd talk to you about it. We're going to help, right? After watching Josh today, I really want to help—a lot maybe, perhaps anonymously even. What do you think?"

"Absolutely!" he replied.

STEP 4 SUMMARY
Giving Makes You Happier

1. Part of the stewardship of money includes giving some of what you make to help others. Devote 10 percent of your income to tithing and an additional amount to other offerings.

2. Giving helps you put your problems in perspective and keeps you focused on how you can help others, instead of only yourself.

3. Give some, no matter how little you have.

4. Make a point of giving not only of your financial income but of your time and talents, too. Seek to serve others in many ways as a part of your life purpose, and look for opportunities to do so.

5. As you make a point of giving in these various ways, no matter how little you feel you have to offer, your overall happiness and success will increase. This is because seeking to fulfill your stewardship and life purpose naturally brings more abundance and happiness into your life.

6. When you need additional income, use your creativity and hard work. Part of financial fitness is taking action to improve things for others, and this often involves conjuring up new incomes.

GOING DEEPER
PART II

FREE ENTERPRISE

Every young person should learn about the importance of free enterprise. This is a system of economics that allows the most freedom and brings the most positive results for people. In the book *Financial Fitness: The Offense, Defense, and Playing Field of Personal Finance*, we learn the following about free enterprise:

History shows the truth of what works, and what doesn't work. There is no bureaucrat or government agency that can make hundreds of millions of choices as well as the regular people can make them.

Moreover, there is no government that can make your choices for you better than you can.

As more people take the enterprising approach to life, whole societies are hugely influenced for good. The collective, individually chosen enterprise of a nation of free people is one of the most powerful forces in all human history.

Invest in yourself by learning to be the kind of person who consistently engages in an enterprising, creative, enthusiastic type of life. Fill your days with enterprise, action, and doing things that matter. And teach your children and the people you work with to do the same.

Free enterprise declines when people become complacent or apathetic, leave things to others or the government, and/or just go to work, watch TV, and go to bed. Become the kind of person and leader who consistently works on your current enterprise. As you do this, and as you help others to do the same, you will have a long-term influence for good.[1]

Help build and improve the free enterprise system by being a leader and a saver and by helping people in need. One of the most effective ways to do this is through business ownership. A nation of enterprisers will always be more prosperous and free than a nation of dependents.

Financially fit people, including youth, learn about free enterprise and do all they can to ensure that it lasts.

(To learn more about free enterprise and how you can help it flourish and spread, read chapters twenty-one through twenty-six of *Financial Fitness: The Offense, Defense, and Playing Field of Personal Finance.*)

INVESTING MONEY

WHAT MOST PEOPLE DON'T KNOW

Invest in yourself.
Your career is the engine of your wealth.
—PAUL CLITHEROE

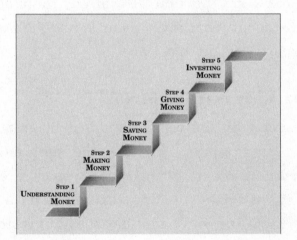

Remember the story about Will from the introduction to this book—you know, the one that emphasized the power of getting a financial education when you're young? This story is a good example of someone who didn't understand, but later learned, what a real investment is.

Investment, especially for children and teens, is not as simple as we tend to think. It's not just about stocks, bonds, mutual funds, or rental properties. In fact, this kind of investment is only a small piece of the puzzle. It only applies to a few people, and it isn't anywhere close to the most important thing about investment for people to be learning at your age—or any age, for that matter.

In fact, when it comes to investing money, there are three main points that need to be addressed. The type of investment that makes the most sense for people in your shoes is *not* the kind we typically think of, and a good talk about what investment is really all about is very important right about now.

Download It in Your Mind!

To begin with, as we've discussed in great detail already, the first and most important type of investment for you to make on a consistent basis is an investment in knowledge and education on financial fitness, leadership, and anything else you need to master to more fully accomplish your life purpose.

> The first and most important type of investment for you to make on a consistent basis is an investment in knowledge and education.

From what we've said already, you know this type of education and learning matters, but we're going to take it a step further. Not only should you see education as a top priority. You should also come to see it as exactly what it is: a powerful and literal investment.

Unfortunately, when most people say "investment," they either mean it very narrowly (for example, stocks and mutual funds) or too vaguely. In fact, if they don't mean their job's built-in investment package, they often mean the purchase of something that is enjoyable to use or that feels worthwhile. This is only a partial definition and can therefore be misleading.

Granted, this definition means a satisfying purchase, but if it isn't going to directly increase your future cash flow in some way, it is *not* an investment. An investment is something you can put time or money into that will directly bring you a lot more time or money in the future.

> **An investment is something you can put time or money into that will directly bring you a lot more time or money in the future.**

So when we say education is an investment, we don't just mean it is satisfying or even that it's worth the money you're spending. We mean it will directly influence how much money you can make in the future. And not all education will help you with this! Some will, but it's important to know the difference.

The number-one principle, then, is this: invest in books, audios, seminars, mentoring, and educational experiences that will increase your financial understanding, wisdom, and leadership education. And always keep saving 20–50 percent or more of all your income.

Be wise about how and where you invest, and don't be afraid to spend money to improve your mind. Benjamin Franklin said, "If a man empties his purse into his head, no man can take it away from him. An investment in knowledge always pays the best interest."[1]

> **Don't be afraid to spend money to improve your mind.**

This is always true, and as a young person, you have a great opportunity to start right from the very beginning. Think back to Will's story and how angry he was when he first started investing in the right kind of financial knowledge and education—because he wished someone had taught him the principles of financial fitness when he was young.

It was a tough road, the more so because he had experienced failures and disappointments that could have been avoided if he had understood the right kind of investment earlier.

While he found hope and was able to make and utilize this type of successful investment at age forty, *you* have the chance to start decades earlier.

As Orrin Woodward said, "When you buy books, it's not an expense; it's an investment." In reality, it is not only an investment; it's the best type of investment for you to make. And now is the best time to start.

> **"When you buy books, it's not an expense; it's an investment."**
> **—Orrin Woodward**

Not only should you *not* be afraid to spend some of your limited funds on good books and audios, and not only should you see doing so as a hugely beneficial investment, but you should seek to get as much financial and leadership education as you can as soon as you can. In fact, this is the main type of investment, if not the only kind, you should be getting involved in for now.

While there may come a time when the other stuff makes sense, you aren't really there yet. This leads us to the second point we need to discuss about teen investment.

Don't Download into the Mud!

To start off, you should understand that most of what people think of as "investing" is actually a bad idea for almost all people who aren't already quite literally "rich."

Robert Kiyosaki says an investor is someone who can afford to lose a quarter of a million dollars overnight in an investment without much of a care. Since most teens aren't in this position, suffice it to say that you shouldn't be trying to be an investor in this generic sense. Don't go throwing your money at the stock market, into real estate, or anywhere else like that.

To put it bluntly, you can't afford to lose it, and you don't know enough yet to *keep from* losing it. Most adults are in the same boat.

Of course you should consult with your financial mentors, but the rule on this, as taught by Chris Brady, Orrin Woodward, and the other founders of LIFE Leadership in the book *Financial Fitness*, is pretty straightforward: "Only invest money you can afford to lose entirely in speculations outside your area(s) of mastery. Only invest a little, if any, in such ventures."[2] Better still, put all your investment into areas you deeply understand and personally control. This takes business ownership to a whole new level. First, owning your own business enables you to make more time and money to do your real purpose in life. Second, investment in your business gives you a lot more control over your investment than any other vehicle.

> **Just knowing you shouldn't invest outside the guidelines presented here may help you avoid making unnecessary mistakes along the way.**

Of course, for now, investment should mean pretty much just books, audios, and seminars to you, but understanding this principle will help you when you get closer to being ready for other investments. And the knowledge you're gaining from these books and materials will directly help your future business. Not to mention, just knowing you shouldn't invest outside these guidelines may help you avoid making unnecessary mistakes along the way.

YOU DON'T HAVE TO *BE* STUPID TO *FEEL* STUPID

Nick had experienced a fantastically abundant summer. It was beautiful! He learned so much from his brother-in-law Jared, selling customer-retention care packages at car dealerships all over the state.

It had been fun starting out just shadowing Jared, watching what he did and listening to how he spoke to the different people. After a while, he started to understand the process, and eventually Jared let him try his hand at selling. It was hard work!

It was amazing how hard it could be just talking to people. Between the not-infrequent rejections and the energy it took to find out if and how their product could really help the person he was talking to, it wasn't just a simple social call. But Nick found it exhilarating.

He loved the work and really enjoyed finding a way to solve people's problems with what he had to offer. It became more than just sales. The whole thing was a workshop on creativity and problem solving. And when he understood the ways to make it all win–win, not only was it fun and educational, but it also paid him a fair amount. He even got a good tan!

Overall, the summer had been a huge success.

And as often happens, now that he had some money tucked away after savings and tithing—way more than he needed to spend—it seemed like all sorts of investment opportunities were popping up. He'd never noticed how many chances to invest in start-up companies and such ventures were out there, but now that he had a little money put away, they seemed to be coming out of the woodwork on all sides.

Nick tried to be smart about how he invested, reading lots of quotes from famous investors on the Internet, but he simply didn't know what he was doing. Then a "once-in-a-lifetime, you-can't-say-no" opportunity came up.

One of his school buddies had found a new, exciting operation that would supposedly triple his initial investment in just four months! The minimum buy-in was $5,000, and after waiting the short amount of time, they'd simply hand him a $15,000 check.

From everything Nick could tell, the group seemed both stable and honest, and fifteen sounded better than five, no matter how you sliced it. He trusted his buddy, and he wanted to look good to his dad and his financial mentors. What better way than to triple his money in a great short-term investment?

The trouble was he only had about $4,000.

But the opportunity is just so good! he said to himself. *How can I make the extra cash?* He knew the drill and understood his power to make money if he needed it, so he brainstormed, planned, and acted.

A week later, between creativity and hard work, he'd figured out a way to make the money stretch until he could realign the funds and afford the buy-in! He didn't touch his savings, but he limited his fun money and had just enough. He couldn't help but feel that the whole thing was an excellent lesson in abundance. He needed the money, he wanted it for something good, and he could figure out a way to get it just in time. So he invested in the project.

Then he waited the four months.

Then seven months.

Then an entire year.

Fourteen months after he'd made the investment, from everything he could tell, his buddy had simply forgotten the scheme, and he never heard from the people again. He was too embarrassed to call his buddy and demand an accounting, and his friend now avoided him anyway.

Nick tried to tell himself not to cry over spilt milk, but since he was now starting his own business and beginning to understand the nature of *real* investment and the principles of financial fitness, it was sometimes hard not to think of great ways to use his original $5,000.

When he finally spoke to his buddy, he listened to a long string of excuses and apologies—but got no money back.

Nick learned a lot from this experience. The lessons on how capable he was at coming up with money when he really wanted it weren't small. But he did find himself

frequently wishing he'd understood the financial principles that would have told him to hold off on that early
"investment."

When people tell you it's a sure thing, it isn't. When
they tell you that you won't have to work for it, they're
wrong. When they tell you that you'll get your money
back plus extra in just four months, they're mistaken.
And when they assure you it's a "once-in-a-lifetime"
opportunity and they "just have to have your money,"
watch out! Financially fit people know that these are all
serious warning signs.

In hindsight, the main thing Nick learned from the
experience was that you don't know what you don't know!
Assuming you understand what's going on and just
feeling comfortable with your ability to make informed
decisions about unfamiliar ventures is a bad idea! He
needed to invest in areas he really understood—areas
of his own business focus where his hard work would
bring success. Everything else was dangerous ground.

For example, remember the Ohio girl who saved a
lot and bought a house to rent for income? If she plans
to make a career in real estate, her investment might
be the right thing. If not, she's playing a risky game—
because even very experienced real estate investors
don't succeed in every deal. Invest in businesses you
know and have a say in.

We're not saying you're stupid to invest beyond your
expertise, but you'll probably *feel* stupid in a few months
or years if you don't realize early on that investment

is complicated and that most people don't know what they're doing.

And frankly, investing of this type is not what you need for quite a while. For now, focus on reading a lot of books and learning as much as you can. Emphasize saving your money, and save as high a percentage as you can.

> **For now, focus on reading a lot of books and learning as much as you can.**

You can also use these years to gain valuable experience by working odd jobs or interning somewhere, all the while learning about the overall operation of the workplace(s), developing sales and people skills, and growing your knowledge of how the world works. "Invest" your early years building a good foundation that you can spend the rest of your life adding to.

Then, when the time is right, keep saving, and focus some of your fun or other post-savings money on investment in your own business—where your experience and daily work will make the difference.

If at any point you think there's an opportunity that does make sense in your situation, beware! Check with your financial mentors, and remember these cautions and guidelines on investing:

- As Chris Brady says, "If they *need* your money for their project, they don't qualify." Be wary of opportunities that *have* to *have* your money in order to function. They might make sense for other reasons, but *not* as an investment. Check with mentors.

- In investment, as in everything, focus on your personal life purpose and mission, not making money. You want investments that further your life purpose, not too-good-to-be-true money-making or get-rich-quick schemes.

- Never invest money you can't afford to lose 100 percent. It's easy to feel like you won't regret it, but if you actually *will*, hold off! If you can't consider it a donation to a cause that matters to you, you shouldn't put your money there. Save it.

- Always, always, always get direct mentoring from truly capable and qualified mentors before you assume you're ready to dive into the world of investment.

- Finally, if you have money to spend on an investment, consider saving it or spending some of it on good books instead. Then *read* them! And this bears repeating: When the time comes, invest in your own business. This is by far the best investment.

> **If you have money to spend on an investment, consider saving it or spending some of it on good books instead.**

INVESTOR MINDSET

The third point we want to address is the idea of developing an investor *mindset*. This means you view the world in general in a slightly different way than most people. To have the right mindset, you seek to make each action, expense, or output of any kind bring you long-term returns in some way. This is huge because even just *trying* to turn everything into a strong, effective investment, instead of a frivolous expenditure, goes a long way toward slashing overall life expenses and increasing the value received from everything you spend.

This is powerful! As you seek to turn your expenses into investments, you will be practicing all sorts of innovation, creativity, and ingenuity—not to mention the fact that you'll probably also find yourself more frequently saying no to things that won't add much value to your life.

In view of the added value you'll create and the unnecessary waste you'll avoid, adopting an investor mindset is truly a powerful thing. To more fully adopt a wise investor mindset, consider the following questions whenever you think about spending money—or time or any other valuable resource—on anything:

1. Am I spending my money on something that will bring back more than I put in?
2. Is this use of money furthering my life purpose?

3. How can I connect this financial choice to my life purpose in a powerful way?

4. How can I change or tweak my planned action to increase the value it gives me in return or the impact it has in my life purpose?

5. Am I valuing return and true worth over short-term fun in the way I look at this financial decision?

6. Am I just buying this to try to impress someone? (If so, stop! Don't buy to impress! It seldom works, and it is always financially unfit.)

7. Is there a way I can reduce the expense or increase the value of this choice through creativity, initiative, innovation, ingenuity, industry, waiting, and so forth?

8. Is there something else I should be using this money for that would be a *better* investment for my future finances and purpose?

9. Is this financial outlay an investment (it will bring me more money) or an expense (once it's spent, it's gone)?

10. How can I turn this expense into an investment?

11. Will this item increase or decrease in value after my initial purchase?

12. Have I talked seriously with my mentor about this?

Asking these questions as you consider financial choices will help you have a more investment-oriented financial lifestyle, and it will also help you avoid making foolish or frivolous financial decisions.

It is certainly important to consult with mentors, seek abundant financial education, and learn more and better ways to increase your investments and decrease your expenses. However, simply asking the right questions before you hand out your cash will get you halfway there.

As you focus on using your money productively to increase it and the value it can bring you, seeking to make your purchases investments rather than expenses, you'll be closer and closer to the kind of investor mindset that turns everything into a powerful tool for your overall financial fitness and the fulfillment of your life purpose.

This is great stuff, and it's simple to start applying right away. From now on, you can simply focus on buying things that will tend to appreciate, increase in value, and add to your success and happiness in life rather than things that will go out with a one-time bang, be forgotten in a week or month, or just sit in the garage or your closet.

In short, to achieve an investor mindset, above all, continuously strive toward that goal. Focus on investing in memories, assets, knowledge, wisdom, and other things that will add to your ability to build your leadership and financial fitness, achieve success in life, and find happiness and fulfillment in your life mission.

THREE TIPS ON INVESTMENT

To recap, there are three main things you need to understand and do when it comes to investment.

The first is to invest in knowledge! Get the book *Turn the Page*.[3] Learn how to read most effectively for success and leadership, and then invest like crazy in good books, audios, and education!

Don't be afraid to invest money on books and educational tools and experiences that will improve your mind and make you much better at fulfilling your purpose and making a meaningful contribution to the world. This has to do with financial education specifically and learning and knowledge in general.

Making an investment in your mind and education is something you will never regret. You might even consider dedicating a portion of your income to building a personal library. But the most important thing about books is to *read* them, think about them, and apply what you learn!

Be as hungry as you can, and get as much education (financial and otherwise) as you can. Doing this will directly enhance your ability to make money and use it in the best ways as well as your ability to affect and influence the world in meaningful ways.

Here are some books to study as part of your financial education. In fact, consider the investment of making them part of your personal leadership library:

1. Chris Brady, *PAiLS: 20 Years from Now, What Will You Wish You Had Done Today?*

2. LIFE Leadership Essentials Series, *Turn the Page: How to Read Like a Top Leader*

3. LIFE Leadership Essentials Series, *Mentoring Matters: Targets, Techniques, and Tools for Becoming a Great Mentor*

4. LIFE Leadership Essentials Series, *Financial Fitness: The Offense, Defense, and Playing Field of Personal Finance*

5. Orrin Woodward, *RESOLVED: 13 Resolutions for LIFE*

6. Robert Kiyosaki, *Cashflow Quadrant: Rich Dad's Guide to Financial Freedom*

7. Oliver DeMille and Shanon Brooks, *Thomas Jefferson Education for Teens*

8. Chris Brady and Orrin Woodward, *Edge*

9. Chris Brady, *Rascal: Making a Difference by Becoming an Original Character*

10. Tim Marks, *Voyage of a Viking: How a Man of Action Can Become a Man of Grace*

11. Claude Hamilton, *Toughen Up!: Basic Training for Leadership and Success*

12. Chris Brady and Orrin Woodward, *Launching a Leadership Revolution: Mastering the Five Levels of Influence*

13. Chris Brady, *A Month of Italy: Rediscovering the Art of Vacation*

14. Orrin Woodward and Oliver DeMille, *LeaderShift: A Call for Americans to Finally Stand Up and Lead*

15. Robert Kiyosaki, *Rich Dad, Poor Dad: What the Rich Teach Their Kids about Money That the Poor and Middle Class Do Not!*

Each of these books will greatly help you in your financial and leadership education.

 The second investment tip is to avoid getting caught up in types of "investment" that you aren't ready for and won't be able to use effectively and valuably. For now, focus on investing in your mind. Avoid the temptation to speculate in other forms of investment, remembering and considering the specific investment guidelines outlined in this book.

And the third tip is to develop an investor mindset. Make a point of seeking ways to turn expenses, action, and all other forms of money outlay into meaningful and productive assets that will give you more than you put in.

Ask yourself the right questions, and always look for creative and powerful ways to turn expenditures into assets. Whenever you can, choose savings over investment and investment over expense. Be willing to say no to anything that won't bring you greater value, wealth, happiness, and fulfillment in your life purpose.

As you learn these three principles of investment and use them in your approach to money and all other valuable resources, you will become more and more financially fit. You will see huge returns and avoid serious financial disappointment and loss.

These principles really work, and the effort they require is more than worth it. And remember to read, read, read! The financial and leadership education you gain now will be one of the most powerful investments you'll ever make. And the returns will keep coming throughout your entire life.

Invest in Becoming a Better Leader!

1. The main type of investment to focus on now is an investment in your mind. Invest in books, audios, seminars, mentoring, and educational experiences that will increase your financial and leadership understanding. Be wise about how and where you invest, but don't be afraid to spend money to improve your mind.

2. Don't get caught up in typical types of investment. Just keep reading books! And seek other work and real-world experiences that will help you build a foundation for life.

3. Don't invest in ventures that *need* your money to function or promise results that sound too good to be true. Walk away!

4. Don't invest money you can't afford to lose 100 percent.

5. Never delve into the world of direct investment without specific counsel from a financially fit and investment-savvy financial mentor.

6. Focus on investing in your mission and your life purpose rather than investing purely to make more money. Save your investment money to put into your own business when the time is right.

7. Develop an investor mindset, always seeking creative and innovative ways to turn expenses into

assets and saying no to unnecessary or frivolous expenses.

8. Remember that successful investors invest in things they really care about, where they have a real say in the outcome.

SPENDING MONEY

WISE LEADERSHIP,
EVEN WHEN YOU'RE YOUNG

Keeping up with the Joneses: Spending money you don't have for things you don't need to impress people you don't like.
—WALTER SLEZAK

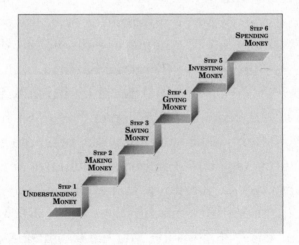

Once you begin to apply the first five steps outlined in this book, you have the relative freedom to spend the rest of your income as you see fit. The idea that you should never spend any money on anything you simply want or think would be fun is actually not true. It's just important to have the firm foundation built by the other five steps before you start spending.

> **The idea that you should never spend any money on anything you simply want or think would be fun is actually not true. It's just important to have the firm foundation built by the other five steps before you start spending.**

This may sound irresponsible until you remember that you are dedicating 60–70 percent of your income specifically to achieving greater financial fitness. Not to mention, you've turned an additional 15 percent into a powerful way to set and achieve goals in life through Targeted Savings.

After that, it really is okay to spend your remaining 15 percent or so on fun and things you want—especially when you take into account your focus on developing an investor mindset and financial fitness. When you know and apply the other principles taught in this book, giving it your 100 percent (or in this case, 85 percent), you have some freedom to enjoy the remainder in the way that best pleases you. Enjoy the blessings that come with your stewardship!

BUT BEWARE...

Your dedication to the other steps of financial abundance means you have the freedom to use your spending money on your wants and desires. Now, let's talk about what this *doesn't* mean.

It does not mean you can cheat the other steps in order to spend more money freely on expenses and consumption.

It does not mean you should start using debt, payment plans, layaway, credit cards, or any other forms of consumer debt to supplement the 5–15 percent you have for fun purchases.

It does not mean you should start throwing away your spending money just because you have it and you can.

It does not mean you should be in the habit of spending money to impress others, look good, or fit in.

It does not mean you should buy worthless or harmful things.

It does not mean you should be at the mercy of advertisers and marketing, buying everything that's offered or seems cool.

It does not mean you should stop planning and strategizing the best ways to spend your money, or paying attention to where it goes and how you can make it go further, to get higher value from it.

It's important to remember that no matter how wisely and well you handle the other 85 percent, you are *still* a steward over the final 15 percent also. There's something it is *meant* for, and that's your fun and fulfillment.

It really is *for* that. But this doesn't mean you should treat it irresponsibly or foolishly.

Even with your fun money, focus on spending it wisely and well on the things that will bring you the most value. Sometimes this means saving until something you want is actually worth it. In any event, do not participate in any of the debt schemes we've mentioned because doing so will inevitably lead to a bad financial situation.

> **Even with your fun money, focus on spending wisely and well on the things that will bring you the most value. Sometimes this means saving until something you want is actually worth it.**

Use your free spending money how you want, but don't put yourself in bondage by using artificial means to buffer your income. If you need your 15 percent to be bigger, find creative ways to make it stretch further or to make your whole 100 percent bigger, and then add more to your savings and giving as well.

BIG BUCKS OR LITTLE PENNIES

There are two main ways people get involved in overspending. The first is infrequent but fairly substantial purchases. In other words, they never buy a hamburger or spend money on little things, but every now and then, they blow the bank on a flat-screen TV or some other big expense.

The other type of overspender is the all-the-time little expenditures person—the one who never buys the flat screen but buys the hamburger at every chance.

The important thing to remember in this is that both types are still overspending! Whether you blow everything on one big expense, and that's all you ever do, or you just can't say no to anything priced under a dollar (or ten), overspending is still incorrect spending.

So pay attention to your tendencies, and guard against whichever type of misspending tempts you. The best way to do this is to set a budget for yourself, including the percentages of your income that go to savings and giving, and stick to it!

Using such a large portion of your income so well is a great check against misspending because as you follow your budget, no matter how much money you spend on electronics or that new leather bag, it's only going to be 15 percent or less of your overall income.

It's okay to indulge in things like hamburgers and music, and even in a flat-screen TV once in a while, so long as you're committed and consistent about being financially fit and using the proper percentages before you make all your purchases. But even in these cases, remember to think like an investor: Is this purchase an asset? If not, how can you use this money on an asset instead?

THE 24-HOUR RULE

Another good idea to help you keep your spending in check and working for you in the best ways is to set a specific dollar amount that makes sense within your personal circumstances and financial situation and never spend more than that (even if you can afford to) without waiting twenty-four hours first. This gives you time to make sure you *really* want it, and it helps you avoid purchases that aren't actually necessary or helpful to you in the long run, even though they might seem good in the moment.

This is about making purchases that actually matter to you, instead of needlessly spending on things that seem good at first but aren't really the best option.

> This is about making purchases that actually matter to you, instead of needlessly spending on things that seem good at first but aren't really the best option.

For example, Orrin and Laurie Woodward were financially successful and were keeping their eyes out for a home to make their "estate." Over years of looking, they visited countless homes that were big, beautiful, luxurious, and elegant—homes that seemed great and were being sold at a decent price. There were many times when they nearly purchased one or another of them. They had the money, and the houses were nice.

But they had a rule that they didn't spend over a certain amount without waiting twenty-four hours to consider the purchase—no matter how much they wanted it. They ended up saying no to a lot of different properties, until they finally found the beautiful Florida estate they now own.

This story teaches two main ideas that can help you shape your spending mindset in the best way to make you more successful, happy, and financially fit. The first important lesson is simply the 24-Hour Rule, which is easy to understand and apply and will help a ton in keeping your purchases meaningful and satisfying.

Your maximum dollar amount for the 24-Hour Rule will depend on how much you actually make and what percentage is left in your 15 percent spending money (or 30 percent if you decide to also use your Targeted Savings). But be sure to consult with your mentor and set one.

For example, let's say your number is $10. Now that you have that set, you know that any time you want to spend more than $10 on something, you have to sit on the purchase for twenty-four hours to make sure you really want it and wouldn't rather save your money or spend it on something else.

This is a simple process that will help you get more value from your money because often, twenty-four hours is enough to decide you didn't really care that much. If you get over it that fast, you're usually better off with the cash than the purchase.

And if you still think it's a good idea and decide to get it after the twenty-four hours, you'll appreciate it that much more, and you'll know you're making a mature decision and not just responding to impulsive emotions.

> **Often, twenty-four hours is enough to decide you didn't really care that much. If you get over it that fast, you're usually better off with the cash than the purchase.**

Sometimes salespeople or advertisements will try to push you into an immediate purchase by making it a once-in-a-lifetime opportunity, but if you know your number and stick to it, you won't be sorry! Don't be pressured into sacrificing your commitments and principles by media marketing schemes.

As Chris Brady put it, "Most people are not in financial trouble because they let the good deal slip away." In most cases, if the deal is that pushy and "now or never," you're better off to be skeptical of it anyway.

> **"Most people are not in financial trouble because they let the good deal slip away."**
> **—Chris Brady**

So set your number and stick to it, no matter what marketing ploys and sales techniques come up.

Delayed Gratification

The other important lesson to learn from Orrin and Laurie's story is the power of delayed gratification. We talked about this principle a little bit earlier, but there's still more to be said.

Sometimes it's better not to spend on purchases, even when you can afford them, so you'll be able to afford even more or better things later. Delayed gratification is the principle of saying no to *good* today so you can have something *great* later.

Because Orrin and Laurie were willing to say no to so many good properties, they were able to afford a really great one when it came along. If they had spent their money on a good house along the way, they wouldn't have had the same freedom when they found what they truly wanted.

This can be applied to big things like a dream house or all sorts of little things. For example, Ruthie grinned as she looked down at her first official paycheck from her first official job! She had worked hard through the summer for the money, and it felt good to have accomplished so much.

After she had taken out the percentages for her financial fitness commitments, she had $30 left over to spend on whatever she wanted! That afternoon, she went to the department store with her best friend, Ashley, and they looked through their two favorite sections: the books and the music CDs.

Ruthie knew she wanted a good book to read, so she picked one she'd been looking for and placed it in the basket. It wasn't an expensive book, so she'd still have around $20 once she got it.

As they looked through the CDs, Ruthie tried to find one that was worth it to her and fit her price. Nothing quite stood out. There were a couple she sort of wanted, but the money she had earned almost seemed too valuable for them, so she decided to hold on to it.

This routine was repeated for several months. Ruthie would pay out just a small portion of her spending money, or none at all, because nothing else seemed worth it to her. Occasionally, friends would ask her to eat out or join them for ice cream. Sometimes she'd join them, but more often, she just ate the lunch her mom had sent with her.

When summer ended, she kept the job after school. And by the end of her first year—after receiving a 50¢ per hour raise eight months in—she had accumulated an extra $300 in spending money that she was free to use however she desired.

That's when Ashley's family decided to take a long-anticipated Disneyland trip, and they invited Ruthie to come along! She'd have to pay for herself, but she'd be safe with them and would have a blast.

Ruthie considered the opportunity for a while to decide if she wanted to spend her money on this—definitely fulfilling the 24-Hour Rule. And since she hadn't said yes to every fast-food run with her friends, she was able to say yes to the Disneyland trip and still have money left over.

Ruthie and Ashley had a fantastic time and made all sorts of memories they'll never forget. They even met one of their favorite actresses there while waiting in line! They took a picture with the actress and sent it to all their friends.

After she got home, Ruthie continued the same approach to her spending money and was able to buy herself a laptop several months later, as she was becoming excited about her writing hobby. Sometimes it was hard to say no to a music CD here and a hamburger there, but she never regretted it! The freedom to use the money on what she really wanted always made up for the sacrifice of the little things she'd forget a minute later.

This is the power of delayed gratification. When you develop the habit of not spending money, even if it's only a little at a time, on things that aren't really worth much and instead delay the gratification for times when it can really bring you value, you will find that your money is worth more and your lifestyle is more fulfilling and productive.

Applying this principle to your spending brings an abundant return. Let's face it: an estate on the beach is better than even a hundred ugly couches, and a trip to Disneyland is better than a whole shelf of CDs.

Go Forth and Spend Wisely!

As we said at the opening of the chapter, when you are living the principles and applying the techniques of financial fitness taught in this book, you really can do whatever you want with your leftover spending money.

It's that simple. If you don't understand the principles or aren't yet living them, there's a lot that can go wrong with your spending.

If you *do* have the right information and tools and you actually use them, no matter what, you will make the right spending decisions, and you can use your fun money for anything you desire!

Since you are consistently saving and following the power of percentages, understanding the perils of debt and overspending, and you are continually seeking the counsel and guidance of good mentors on the *best* purchases out there, you will be in a great place financially.

> **When you are dedicating the 85 percent of your income to the other things taught in this book, the money allotted for fun *actually* goes toward fun! You really get to use it! Enjoy!**

When you are dedicating the 85 percent of your income to the other things taught in this book, the money allotted for fun *actually* goes toward fun! You really get to use it! Enjoy!

Feel free to brainstorm and strategize the ways to spend this money that will be the *most* fun for you. Or not! You can also save it for even more fun later. Take us at our word when we say "free spending."

Learn these principles, and then follow them! Don't dabble or do them halfway. Commit and stay consistent! When you do, spending money isn't a danger or a taboo. It's just another piece of the puzzle—another step to abundance!

Find out what your life purpose is. Get right with God, and know what He wants and expects from you. Learn the important principles in all areas of life (including finances) that will make you a better steward and a more successful person, and then *apply* them!

Fulfill your responsibility as a steward and serve others in all things! As you do this, enjoy the blessings of your stewardship and embrace the journey you're on.

And remember, be content to live the life you've always

> **Be content to live the life you've always wanted, and let God worry about impressing others.**

wanted, and let God worry about impressing others. If being financially flabby somehow impresses some people, they're not the people who deserve to be impressed. You will have a much happier life as you stay financially fit.

Follow the Steps—They Work!

1. Live steps 1–6 perfectly!
2. Have fun spending the right percentage of your income in the way that makes you happiest.
3. Beware of overspending. Find out if you're a "big, one-time purchase" spender or a "break the bank with nickels" buyer, or both, and combat your tendencies. Set your free-spending budget and keep to it.
4. Set a specific dollar amount that makes sense to you and your mentors, and never spend more than that without waiting twenty-four hours.
5. Apply the principle of delayed gratification in your spending, and don't be afraid to *not* spend when there's nothing worth your money, knowing that something will come up later. Say no to the *good* today so you can have the *great* later.
6. Don't spend money trying to impress others. Financial flabbiness is never impressive.
7. Find your purpose, fulfill your stewardship, apply the principles, and serve!

GOING DEEPER
PART III

TEN FINANCIAL DANGER ZONES

Another thing we want to warn you about in the realm of spending is what Chris Brady calls the "Ten Danger Zones of Finance." We're not saying you should never ever use money for these things; in fact, many of them are important and good, at the right time. However, it's easy to mess up in all these zones, and doing that can easily mean huge financial consequences.

So when it comes to any of these danger zones, be wary. Make sure to consult with a good mentor, and pay attention to the risk there.

It might seem as if some of these don't apply to you yet, and that may be the case. But the whole point is to be able to recognize them as danger zones *before* the danger actually bites off your head. So learn what they are now, and if they *do* come up later in your life, know how dangerous they are and act with extreme caution. Remember, you are building a foundation of principles to support you for the rest of your life!

The danger zones are listed below:

1. **Taxes.** There's often not much you can do about this, except to make sure you know who and what you're voting for and to vote wisely. Still, this is an area where not being financially fit and responsible can really leave you in a tight spot. Always pay your honest taxes. Be smart about saving for taxes when you start your own business, since you might not have taxes automatically withheld whenever you pay yourself. And know that one of the best strategies for reducing the amount of taxes you'll have to pay is to own a business. This is because governments realize that businesses are important for the economy, so they provide incentives or tax deductions for certain expenses.

    For now, just be aware that you will spend a great deal on taxes over the course of your life, so you'll want to know something about them and get good advisers in this area.

2. **Home ownership.** It can be great to own your own home, but only when it actually is yours! Especially now, don't feel like you have to be in a rush to achieve the lifestyle your parents and grandparents worked a lifetime to obtain.

    It's better to rent someone else's house than to put yourself in financial peril with too much debt just to "own" your own.

    There are lots of advantages to renting and plenty of disadvantages to premature home ownership. Don't make the mistake of assuming "mine" is always better, especially when debt financing is involved. When it comes to home ownership, be very strategic.

3. **Divorce.** There are many reasons why this is a dangerous area, and financial loss is more than just a small part. When choosing your life's mate, do just that: choose for life!

4. **Credit cards.** This is one of the places where learning the principles when you're young helps the most. Let's put it very clearly: Credit card debt ruins marriages, families, businesses, and lives! Avoid it like the plague.

    Credit cards can be used responsibly, for example, as ready cash or to make cash back or rewards points. But if you aren't paying off your balance every month, you are *not* using credit correctly. Using credit cards to "build credit" almost always leads to more debt, so be extremely careful and guarded about the way you view and use credit cards. Don't be afraid to *not* get them or even to cut them up!

5. **Lawsuits.** Many people think they're going to win big and be financially set for life if they get involved in the right lawsuit. Don't be deceived. In most cases, you're going to lose a lot more than you win, not to mention waste time and energy in a dead-end pursuit. Make a point of avoiding unnecessary lawsuits whenever you can!

6. **Insurance.** Uninsured items that really ought to be insured are a massive danger zone. Meet with financial mentors, and just pay the premium! Of course you shouldn't go around insuring small or unimportant things, but not insuring the right things is playing with fire. Get advice from your parents on what does or doesn't need to be insured—especially when you leave for college or work.

7. **Seeking status.** When you start dedicating your finances, or any of your valuable resources, to seeking status (in other words,

attempting to impress others), you're opening a huge can of worms—a virtually bottomless one. This is one of the easiest ways to lose everything and live a truly miserable life.

Consider the quote at the beginning of this chapter, and *stop* spending money you don't have on things you don't want to impress people you don't like! Find out what you really care about in life, and dedicate your resources to that instead.

8. **College.** Most people today think that college is the best or only good option for anyone who wants a successful life. Know that this is not the case, and there are a lot of financial and other factors involved.

    Know your stuff, know what you actually want, and consult with parents and mentors in deciding whether and where you should go to college and how to pay for it. College can be a good investment if it is right for you and you attend for the right reasons and in the right way. But don't just assume it's the best choice (or the only one), and don't use debt on it. Many people spend decades trying to pay back student loans that did them very little good.

9. **Addictions.** Like status seeking, addictions are a sinkhole, both financially and otherwise.

152 FINANCIAL FITNESS FOR TEENS

Avoid them, and seek help and healing where necessary. The best plan is to stay away from anything and everything addictive. Just don't start!

10. **Investments.** We've already addressed investments in the last chapter, but remember that you don't know everything about investing! It's better to invest in yourself and your business, where you have experience and a real say and stake in the outcome of each venture, than to throw your money at so-called moneymaking schemes you don't understand and can't really influence (even when people promise you a sure thing).

Get good advice from the right financial mentors before you spend anything! Acting wisely in each of these zones can mean the difference between success and ruin in many cases, so don't be flaky on this.

Recognizing and correctly handling financial danger zones is an important aspect of financial fitness. And as you seek mentoring and counsel on these issues, instead of relying on your own gut feelings or the luck of the draw, you'll be achieving higher levels of financial understanding and wisdom to properly deal with future situations.

WHICH GENERATION ARE YOU?

It's never too late to have a happy childhood.
—TOM ROBBINS

The generation that went through the Great Depression understood things that we simply can't with our limited experience. They knew what it felt like to have everything they understood, knew, and expected fall apart and crumble before their eyes, and they were never the same because of it.

They experienced what it felt like to go to the bank and find the doors chained shut, with their money still inside. To hear the president of the United States announce it was a "bank holiday" and have the banks not open again for a long time. To see everyone they loved lose their jobs and go broke. People lost their money, businesses, and homes.

Many of them became cynical and hardened as a result of their experiences. They understood on a deep and personal level what it was like to go without. And so they became naturally very conservative with their money and their possessions. They saved and saved.

> It isn't wrong for you to enjoy the blessings and abundance of your day, but make it a point to understand and appreciate the deep inner struggle and familiarity with sacrifice and hardship of those who lived through the Great Depression or other tough times.

If you've ever laughed at your grandma—or your great-grandma—for saving Ziploc bags, plasticware, or cottage cheese containers, understand that her reasons aren't wrong or even silly. It isn't wrong for you to enjoy the blessings and abundance of your day, but make it a point to understand and appreciate the deep inner struggle and familiarity with sacrifice and hardship that led her to these seemingly comical habits.

Her generation went through extreme financial difficulty, and so they know the importance of saving. Because of this, they saved greatly. And most of your

grandparents and great-grandparents saved and accumulated their whole lives and eventually left what they
had built up to their children.

In some cases, this was a lot; in others, not so much.
Sometimes it took the form of jewelry collections or
land. Other times, it was cash folded into the pages
of books in libraries full of thousands of dollars. Some
stuffed coins under mattresses or kept accounts, bonds,
and safe deposit boxes crammed with money. Some left
large sums of money, even whole fortunes and financial
legacies to last their children's entire lives.

Sadly, history shows that they left it to a generation
who—rather than continuing to save and accumulate—
mostly spent it all. In the end, those who inherited all
these savings have very little savings. And today, they
are raising a generation of people who are often behind
on their mortgage and can barely pay the minimums on
their maxed-out credit cards.

THE WAR YOU FACE

We're hoping this isn't your particular circumstance,
and since you have this book now, your parents have
probably already taken steps toward becoming financially fit themselves. But even if you're one of the blessed
ones, that generation—the one that can't afford its own
debt—is the one that's raising yours.

This is where we are right now.

Herbert Hoover said, "Older men declare war. But it
is youth that must fight and die."[1] This is the reality of

the world you and your generation are inheriting. You

> **"Older men declare war. But it is youth that must fight and die."**
> **—Herbert Hoover**

are left to struggle, thanks to the mistakes, false information, and bad choices of generations that preceded you. You have to pay the debt and interest on food you never ate, houses you never lived in, consumer goods that have long since been broken and sent away in dumpsters, boats you never took out on the waves, and taxes that paid for things the government bought long before you ever got (or will get) a job yourself.

Unfortunately, this is how history has always unfolded. And the irony of the whole thing is that the elders can't seem to decide whether the youth are a bunch of losers, rebels, and entitled upstarts or the light and hope of the future.

If you're in your teens, you've probably heard your generation described in both ways. Interestingly, this isn't new. The older generations have always had something to say about the failings, laziness, and arrogance of the younger ones.

Two Opposing Views of Youth

Consider this quote attributed to Socrates about the youth of his day:

The children now love luxury. They have bad manners, contempt for authority; they show disrespect for elders and love chatter in place of exercise....They no longer rise when elders enter a room. They contradict their parents, chatter before company, gobble up dainties at the table, cross their legs, and tyrannize their teachers.[2]

Sound familiar? That's what he thought of "the youth these days" back in the sixth century BC. (It's funny how he liked that word *chatter*.)

Yet the other most common historical observation about youth is that they are full of potential and are our best hope for future excellence, prosperity, freedom, and success.

Consider this quote from Confucius, who lived around the same time as Socrates: "A youth is to be regarded with respect. How do we know that his future will not be equal to our present?"[3] It is silently implied that it could even be much greater.

As for us, we think your generation will do many great things, and it is up to you to prove us right. But you're not going to do it very well unless you live a life of exemplary financial fitness—and show others how to do the same. For example, just passing this book along to all your friends and peers could be a powerful way to help your whole generation! Use it as birthday gifts, holiday gifts, and gifts for no reason—except that everyone you care about really needs to read it.

And when you give them this book or recommend it to them, tell them why it is so important to you. Tell them you are living the principles of financial fitness, and invite them to do the same. For your generation, this is absolutely essential to success.

The world has always been confused about whether the youth are total failures who don't appreciate what they have *or* the perfect people to make the future wonderful and glorious.

> **The world has always been confused about whether the youth are total failures who don't appreciate what they have *or* the perfect people to make the future wonderful and glorious.**

Interestingly, both are right. The elders aren't always wrong when they say youth is wasted on the young. The fact is the youth have experienced less and know less, so they tend to appreciate less and *do* less about it.

The fact that you haven't lived through your own Great Depression makes this generation far less likely to learn and apply the lessons of savings, even with the potential of youth.

Yet the potential is *still there*! This is why the positive future is still true—because youth *can* learn from the experiences of past generations, and they have the potential and ability to make the right adjustments and developments to change the world in big ways.

Your generation, as all that have gone before, has always been on the balance between waste and hope, leaning and eventually choosing one direction or the other as you live your lives.

Your elders fear you'll never take advantage of your opportunity to make a difference, and they often loudly express their cynicism and doubt. Yet they are secretly hoping that this generation—*your* generation—will be full of young people who rise to the occasion. We believe you will.

We really do!

You've inherited a financial war between waste, debt, and financial flabbiness on one side and success, happiness, and financial fitness on the other. The world threatens to break you if you choose financial flabbiness. You've inherited debts that put your generation behind in the race to begin with.

> **The youthful generation has always been on the balance between waste and hope, leaning and eventually choosing one direction or the other as they live their lives.**

But now you have the opportunity to be an effective and authentic leader and make a better future for yourself and generations to come. Your example of financial fitness matters!

WHICH GENERATION ARE YOU?

What about you, personally? Will you be one who wastes away in entitlement and laziness or one who shines the light of the future?

Will you continue the spiral from fortune to nothing to debt and beyond, or will you choose to pay the price to win this war and live a financially fit life? Will you set the example and help others follow it?

The beauty in all this is that you won't just be fighting and dying for an old man's war. If you choose to take on this battle, to pay this price, not only will you bring a brighter future to the world, but you will live to experience increased personal happiness, financial success, and leadership yourself.

This isn't one of those deals where we're asking you to make the ultimate sacrifice, all for the sake of someone else. We're asking you to increase your own personal happiness, prosperity, and success and, in so doing, to show others how to do the same. Now that's leadership!

If you decide to fill the best possible role of this generation and be the hope of the future by becoming financially fit yourself and passing the principles to others through your various stewardships, you will reap the rewards.

We're asking you to choose personal excellence and financial fitness—and along with these, personal success and happiness. We can't repeat this enough! Financial fitness will bring you blessings in every part of your life.

You don't have to say yes to this challenge, but you'll be glad if you do! Deciding to take this journey will help bring needed changes to our world, and it is also vitally important to your own hopes and dreams. You really do

> **Financial fitness will bring you blessings in every part of your life.**

have all the power to make a huge difference in your own life and in the lives of countless others.

So again, we ask you: Which generation are you? The choice is yours.

TWO ROADS DIVERGE

If you choose the path of financial fitness, the principles in this book are the key. They are few and simple, but they work and work powerfully. If you follow them, you'll find financial fitness and success. If you don't, you won't. It really is that simple because these principles really are that powerful.

If you start saving 20–50 percent or more of everything you make right now, and keep doing it for the rest of your life, you'll experience financial fitness that few people (including adults) ever will. If you consistently tithe and generously give to those in need, you'll feel untold happiness and fulfillment because you'll be living a valuable life—one that truly helps people.

If you combine your life purpose with your career, own your own business, and create residual income that gives you control over your time and finances, you'll have the time and resources to do genuinely great things and exert great leadership in your life. It's the Benjamin Franklin path to greatness.

If you keep a saver/investor mindset instead of wasting your resources on things that are quickly gone, you'll build up increased personal discipline, stature, and influence. You'll naturally become a leader.

If reading, listening to informative audios, and learning are central investments in your life, you'll naturally become the best leader you are capable of being—and this will significantly benefit many people. In short, if you live the few principles of financial fitness covered in this little book, you'll almost surely be one of the stronger, more effective, and better-funded people of your generation.

As a result, you'll do a lot more to build society, serve others, and make a positive difference in the world through your work, family, relationships, example, and leadership. Financial fitness will be a great blessing to you, and you will be a great blessing to many people.

Start now. Apply the principles of financial fitness, and never stop. You'll have a better life, and so will the thousands of people you touch as you work, serve, and lead.

Right now, this is such a small choice, but the consequences will be enormous. So choose wisely—because as a financially fit person, you will do much more to improve the world than you will if you opt to spend much of your life struggling just to pay the bills.

By starting now, you are choosing a life of great service and leadership. And that's a choice worth making—for everyone. Starting today. Starting with *you*.

NOTES

Introduction: Why Don't Schools Teach This?

1   LIFE Leadership, *Financial Fitness: The Offense, Defense, and Playing Field of Personal Finance* (Flint, MI: Obstaclés Press, 2013).

Step 1: Understanding Money
Focus on the Basics

1   Oscar Wilde, *Oscar Wilde's Wit & Wisdom: A Book of Quotations* (Mineola, NY: Dover Thrift Editions), p. 49.

2   J.R.R. Tolkien, *Lord of the Rings*, three-part series, including *The Fellowship of the Ring* (July 29, 1954), *The Two Towers* (November 11, 1954), and *The Return of the King* (October 20, 1955), written in stages between 1937 and 1949 (UK: George Allen & Unwin).

3   LIFE Leadership, *Financial Fitness*, pp. 48, 72, 265.

4   LIFE Leadership Essentials Series, *Mentoring Matters: Targets, Techniques, and Tools for Becoming a Great Mentor* (Flint, MI: Obstaclés Press, 2013).

Step 2: Making Money
The Ownership Rule: Owners Rule

1   Carlos Ruiz Zafón, *The Shadow of the Wind* (New York: The Penguin Press, 2004), p. 371.

2   Oliver DeMille, *FreedomShift* (The Center for Social Leadership, 2010).

3   Chris Brady, *PAiLS: 20 Years from Now, What Will You Wish You Had Done Today?* (Flint, MI: Obstaclés Press, 2013).

4   Robert T. Kiyosaki with Sharon L. Lechter, CPA, *Rich Dad's Cashflow Quadrant: Rich Dad's Guide to Financial Freedom* (New York: Warner Books Inc., 2000).

5   Rob Berger, "Top 100 Money Quotes of All Time," *Forbes*, posted 4/30/2014 at 9:01 a.m., www.forbes.com/sites/robertberger/2014/04/30/top-100-money-quotes-of-all-time/.

6   Marvel, *The Avengers*, story by Zak Penn and Joss Whedon, screenplay by Joss Whedon, directed by Joss Whedon, released May 4, 2012 (USA).

Going Deeper, Part I: Four Ways to Make Money

1   Kiyosaki with Lechter, *Cashflow Quadrant*.

Step 3: Saving Money

Percentage Power!

1   LIFE Leadership, *Financial Fitness*.

2   Ibid., pp. 26, 39, 53, 72, 265.

Step 4: Giving Money

Smile Big ☺

1   See Mark 12:41-44 and Luke 21:1-4.

Going Deeper, Part II: Free Enterprise

1   LIFE Leadership, *Financial Fitness*, p. 237-238.

Step 5: Investing Money

What Most People Don't Know

1   Benjamin Franklin, as quoted in *George S. Clason's The Richest Man in Babylon: A 52 Brilliant Ideas Interpretation* by Karen McCreadie (Oxford, UK: Infinite Ideas Limited, 2009), p. 53.

2   LIFE Leadership, *Financial Fitness*, 152, 160, 268.

3   LIFE Leadership Essentials Series, *Turn the Page: How to Read Like a Top Leader* (Flint, MI: Obstaclés Press, 2013).

Conclusion: Which Generation Are You?

1   President Herbert Hoover, in a speech given in 1944, as quoted in "Herbert Hoover" article from the Editors of Encyclopædia Britannica, last updated August 25, 2014, copyright 2014 Encyclopædia Britannica, Inc., www.britannica.com/topic/271392/supplemental-information.

2   Attributed to Socrates by Plato, according to William L. Patty and Louise S. Johnson, *Personality and Adjustment* (McGraw-Hill, 1953), p. 277. See also "Respectfully Quoted: A Dictionary of Quotations," 1989, copyright 1993-2014 Bartleby.com, accessed August 25, 2014, www.bartleby.com/73/195.html.

3   Confucius, *The Analects of Confucius: Confucian Analects the Great Learning the Doctrine of the Mean*, Book IX: TSZE HAN, Chapter XXII, translated by James Legge, from the series *The Chinese Classics: Confucius* (CreateSpace Indpendent Publishing Platform, 2014), p. 27.

Other Books in the
LIFE Leadership Essentials Series

Financial Fitness: The Offense, Defense, and Playing Field of Personal Finance **with Introduction by Chris Brady and Orrin Woodward – $21.95**
If you ever feel that you're too far behind and can't envision a better financial picture, you are so WRONG! You need this book! The *Financial Fitness* book is for everyone at any level of wealth. Just like becoming physically or mentally fit, becoming financially fit requires two things: knowing what to do and taking the necessary action to do it. Learn how to prosper, conserve, and become fiscally fantastic. It's a money thing, and the power to prosper is all yours!

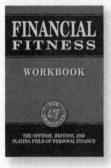

Financial Fitness Workbook **– $7.95**
Economic affairs don't have to be boring or stressful. Make managing money fun in a few simple steps. Use this workbook to get off to a great start and then continue down the right path to becoming fiscally fabulous! Discover exactly where all of your money actually goes as you make note of all your expenditures. Every page will put you one step closer to financial freedom, so purchase the *Financial Fitness Workbook* today and get budgeting!

Mentoring Matters: Targets, Techniques, and Tools for Becoming a Great Mentor **with Foreword by Orrin Woodward – $19.95**
Get your sticky notes ready for all the info you're about to take in from this book. Do you know what it means to be a *great* mentor? It's a key part of successful leadership, but for most people, the necessary skills and techniques don't come naturally. Educate yourself on all of the key targets, techniques, and tools for becoming a magnificent mentor with this easy-to-apply manual. Your leadership success will be forever increased!

Turn the Page: How to Read Like a Top Leader with **Introduction by Chris Brady – $15.95**
Leaders are readers. But there are many ways to read, and leaders read differently than most people do. They read to learn what they need to know, do, or feel, regardless of the author's intent or words. They see past the words and read with the specific intent of finding truth and applying it directly in their own lives. Learn how to read like a top leader so you'll be better able to emulate their success. Applying the skills taught in *Turn the Page* will impact your life, career, and leadership abilities in ways you can't even imagine. So turn the page and start reading!

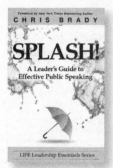

SPLASH!: A Leader's Guide to Effective Public Speaking with **Foreword by Chris Brady – $15.95**
For many, the fear of giving a speech is worse than the fear of death. But public speaking can be truly enjoyable *and* a powerful tool for making a difference in the lives of others. Whether you are a beginner or a seasoned orator, this book will help you transform your public speaking to a whole new level of leadership influence. Learn the SPLASH formula for great public speaking that will make you the kind of speaker and leader who makes a SPLASH—leaving any audience, big or small, forever changed—every time you speak!

The Serious Power of Fun with **Foreword by Chris Brady – $15.95**
Life got you down? Feeling like life isn't much fun is a bad place to be. Fun matters. It is serious business and a source of significant leadership power. Without it, few people maintain the levels of inspired motivation and sustained effort that bring great success. So put a smile back on your face. Discover how to make every area of life more enjoyable and turn any situation into the right kind of fun. Learn to cultivate a habit of designed gratification—where life just keeps getting better—and *laugh your way to increased success* with *The Serious Power of Fun!*

Wavemakers: How Small Acts of Courage Can Change the World **with Foreword by Chris Brady – $15.95**
Every now and then, extraordinary individuals come along who make huge waves and bring about permanent change in the lives of so many that society as a whole is forever altered. Discover from the examples of the various "Wavemakers" showcased in this book how you can make waves of your own and change the world for the better!

Dealing with Difficult People **with Foreword by Chris Brady – $15.95**
How many times have you felt like banging your head against the wall trying to figure out how to deal with a routinely difficult person, whether at work or in your personal life? You can't control others, but you can control how you handle them. Learn about the seven main types of difficult people and the Five-Step Peace Process, and equip yourself to understand why people behave the way they do, break the cycle of frustration, and turn your interactions into healthy, productive experiences. "You are going to encounter difficult people. Plan on it. Prepare for it. Become good at it."

Subscriptions and
Products from
LIFE Leadership

Rascal Radio Subscription – $49.95 per month
Rascal Radio by LIFE Leadership is the world's first online personal development radio hot spot. Rascal Radio is centered on LIFE Leadership's 8 Fs: Faith, Family, Finances, Fitness, Following, Freedom, Friends, and Fun. Subscribers have unlimited access to **hundreds and hundreds** of audio recordings that they can stream endlessly from both the **LIFE Leadership website** and the **LIFE Leadership Smartphone App.** Listen to one of the preset stations or customize your own based on speaker or subject. Of course, you can easily skip tracks or "like" as many as you want. And if you are listening from the website, you can purchase any one of these incredible audios.

Let Rascal Radio provide you with **life-changing information to help you live the life you've always wanted!**

The LIFE Series – $50.00 per month
Here's where LIFE Leadership began—with the now famously followed 8 Fs: Family, Finances, Fitness, Faith, Following, Freedom, Friends, and Fun. This highly recommended series offers a strong foundation on which to build and advance in every area of your daily life. The timeless truths and effective strategies included will reignite passion and inspire you to be your very best. Transform your  life for the better and watch how it will create positive change in the lives of those around you. Subscribe today and have the time of your LIFE!

Series includes 4 audios and 1 book monthly and is also available in Spanish and French.

The LLR (Launching a Leadership Revolution) Series – $50.00 per month
There is no such thing as a born leader. Based on the *New York Times* bestseller *Launching a Leadership Revolution* by Chris Brady and Orrin Woodward, this series focuses on teaching leadership skills at every level. The principles and specifics taught in the LLR Series will equip you with all the tools you need for business advancement, community influence, church impact, and even an advantage in your home life. Topics include: leadership, finances, public speaking, goal setting, mentoring, game planning, accountability and tracking of progress, levels of motivation and influence, and leaving a personal legacy. Will you be ready to take the lead when you're called? Subscribe now and learn how to achieve effective confidence skills while growing stronger in your leadership ability.

Series includes 4 audios and 1 leadership book monthly.

The AGO (All Grace Outreach) Series – $25.00 per month
We are all here together to love one another and take care of each other. But sometimes in this hectic world, we lose our way and forget our true purpose. When you subscribe to the AGO Series, you'll gain the valuable support and guidance that every Christian searches for. Nurture your soul, strengthen your faith, and find answers to better understand God's plan for your life, marriage, and children.

Series includes 1 audio and 1 book monthly.

The Edge Series – $10.00 per month
You'll cut in front of the rest of the crowd when you get the *Edge*. Designed for those on the younger side of life, this hard-core, no-frills series promotes self-confidence, drive, and motivation. Get advice, timely information, and true stories of success from interesting talks and fascinating people. Block out the noise around you and learn the principles of self-improvement at an early age. It's a gift that will keep on giving from parent to child. Subscribe today and get a competitive *Edge* on tomorrow.

Series includes 1 audio monthly.

Financial Fitness Subscription – $10.00 per month for 12 months

If you found the *Financial Fitness Pack* life-changing and beneficial to your bank account, then you'll want even more timely information and guidance from the Financial Fitness Subscription. It's designed as a continuing economic education to help people develop financial discipline and overall knowledge of how their money works. Learn how to make financial principles your financial habits. It's a money thing, and it always pays to be cash savvy.

Subscription includes 1 audio monthly.

Financial Fitness Pack – $99.99

Once and for all, it's time to free yourself from the worry and heavy burden of debt. Decide today to take an honest look at your finances by learning and applying the simple principles of financial success. The *Financial Fitness Pack* provides you with all the tools needed to get on a path to becoming fiscally fantastic!

Pack includes the Financial Fitness *book, a companion workbook, and 8 audio recordings.*